Praise for *Homespun Gifts from the Heart*

"Don't have an ounce of crafter's blood coursing through your veins? Not to worry! *Homespun Gifts from the Heart* will give you the ideas, how-tos, and confidence you need to increase your gift-giving standard and at the same time ease the economic strain. For me, the only thing better than making a gift is to receive one that's homemade. A homemade gift eliminates the worry that maybe I didn't spend enough, and in its place sends the message, 'You mean so much to me, I'm giving you a piece of my heart.'"

Mary Hunt, editor and founder, *Cheapskate Monthly* Newsletter, and best-selling author

"Is your heart for giving often bigger than your budget? Has a busy schedule crowded out time for thoughtful gestures? *Homespun Gifts from the Heart* is filled with hundreds of surprisingly simple ideas for creating priceless presents to show someone you care. What better way to touch people than with loving gifts made by our own hands?"

Lisa Whelchel, author of
Creative Correction and *The Facts of Life and Other Lessons My Father Taught Me*

"Here's help for the creative and not-so-creative woman who yearns to put her heart into the gifts she shares with others! Practical, fun, and inspiring, you'll find help for transferring your love into tangible gifts of love in *Homespun Gifts from the Heart.*"

Elisa Morgan, president and CEO,
MOPS International

"*Homespun Gifts from the Heart* is a book women have been waiting for, a book filled with great ideas and recipes that are fun, quick, and easy. It is great for adults, children, grandparents, and MOPS craft gifts!"

Emilie Barnes, best-selling author of
The 15-Minute Organizer and
If Teacups Could Talk

"I don't think there is a better book available on the subject of homemade gifts. These ladies are the queens of creativity! They have packed their book with imaginative ideas that are very affordable—and even give you ready-made gift tags to copy. Your gifts can now be warm and personal."

Jonni McCoy, author of *Miserly Moms,*
Miserly Meals, and *Frugal Families*

"Finally a book that brings the heart of gift giving back to where it should be. *Homespun Gifts from the Heart* provides ideas for thoughtful, creative, easy gifts that will make the recipient feel valued and loved."

Donna Otto, author of *The Gentle Art of Mentoring* and *Get More Done in Less Time*

HOMESPUN GIFTS *from the* HEART

HOMESPUN GIFTS *from the* HEART

MORE THAN 200 GREAT GIFT IDEAS ❧ 250 PHOTO-READY GIFT TAGS ❧ CLEAR & EASY DIRECTIONS

Karen Ehman, Kelly Hovermale, & Trish Smith

Fleming H. Revell

A Division of Baker Book House Co
Grand Rapids, Michigan 49516

Published by Fleming H. Revell
a division of Baker Book House Company
P.O. Box 6287, Grand Rapids, MI 49516-6287
www.bakerbooks.com

Printed in the United States of America

Library of Congress Cataloging-in-Publication Data
Ehman, Karen, 1964–
    Homespun gifts from the heart : more than 200 great gift ideas, 250 photo-ready gift tags, clear & easy directions / Karen Ehman, Kelly Hovermale & Trish Smith.
       p.   cm.
    ISBN 0-8007-5870-6
    1. Handicraft. 2. Cookery. 3. Gifts. I. Hovermale, Kelly, 1963–   II. Smith, Trish, 1969–   III. Title.
TT157.E434 2003
745.5—dc21   2003043218

On the cover: The recipe for the Michigan Dried Cherry-Cashew bars (pictured top right) is on page 31 and the gift tag is on page 141. Creative gift-wrapping paper ideas (pictured left, top and bottom) can be found in chapters 9 and 10. Themes for gift-giving (as pictured bottom right) are overviewed in chapter 1, with specific ideas on bringing in the outdoors in chapter 7.

"Every good and perfect gift is from above, coming down from the Father . . . who does not change like shifting shadows."

JAMES 1:17

To our heavenly Father, the One who gave us the greatest gift of all: salvation through His Son, Jesus Christ.

And to the most precious gifts we've received this side of heaven: our husbands and children. A heartfelt thanks to you for support and patience while we spent endless hours at the computer, chatting on the phone, or mixing up yet another kitchen concoction for you to sample.

We love you:
Todd, Mackenzie, Mitchell, and Spencer Ehman
Greg, Steven, Austin, Jonathan, and Autumn Hovermale
Doug and Zach Smith

CONTENTS

1

GIVING *from the* HEART — *for the* HEART

. . . .

ow would you describe the perfect gift? The one that says, "You're special"; "You're loved and cherished"; "You matter and here's why." Such a gift probably wouldn't be that one-size-fits-all item, the certificate to a catalog, or the predictable tie for Dad, or perfume for Mom. Nor would it be a generic, cookie-cutter-type gift or trendy product of the season picked up on a quick trip to the mall. No, those gifts say something more like, "I needed to get you something, and this fit into my busy schedule."

The unforgettable gift, however, is the one that's personal, the one that says: "You're worth it—worth the time, worth the effort, worth the thought." It's

- the basket of mouthwatering muffins tied with a favorite-colored bow for your frazzled friend
- a nostalgic, feel-good movie slipped into a bright sack with a fun mug and aromatic tea for a neighbor who is shut in on a wintry day
- turkey noodle soup mix, layered beautifully in an antique jar, for the aunt who's just hosted Thanksgiving dinner for the clan

While a perfect gift is unique and hand-selected with love and attention, it's not necessarily handmade. This book will show you just what that means. With more than 200 ideas for creative, memorable, encouraging, homespun gifts you'll find all kinds of inspiration and how-tos for pulling together something lovely and unforgettable. And you won't need a glue gun in one hand and recipe card in the other.

A Word to the Craft-Challenged

You need not love to sew, be the craft queen of your circle of friends, or have a lot of art smarts to create the perfect gift.

We know! As coauthors and friends we couldn't be more different. Kelly and Trish can work wonders with all sorts of arts and crafts supplies, and they love to sew. They can spot a darling pair of curtains and head home to the sewing machine saying, "We can make that!"

Karen, however, is quite craft impaired. The thought of picking up a glue gun sends chills down her spine—and when she spies a lovely set of curtains, her instinct is to head home, whip out her VISA card, and exclaim, "I can order that!"

A child showed Karen that you don't need to rely on catalog orders and credit cards for extraordinary gifts. One day toward the end of Karen's third pregnancy, when she was napping, her six-year-old left a gift by her bed: a little coaster under a cup of mint tea. Made from scrap material trimmed by pinking shears, the coaster was simply but sweetly stitched with bright thread and buttons for ornaments. An accompanying note read:

Dear Mom,

Thank you for having
another baby for our family.
I love you.

From Mackenzie

The gift itself was small, the love behind it strong, and the timing perfect. Karen thought about the materials used (just little things on hand) and the preparation time, which was as brief as her catnap. What took so little time has remained a lasting memory. The lesson Karen learned was clear: If her six-year-old daughter could make a priceless gift, then she could too.

The Heart of the Matter

Whether you're a Kelly, a Trish, or a Karen, the first step to making perfect gifts is to rouse your creative juices, and one of the best ways is to begin by thinking in terms of themes.

For instance, does someone on your gift list love to garden? Do you know a person who sits for hours with seed catalogs or dreamily talks about what to plant in spring and pull at harvesttime?

Why not make your next gift to that person a large basket or miniature wheelbarrow filled with seeds, herbs, a pair of gardening gloves, a trowel, small terra-cotta pots, and herb-scented hand lotion or soap to use after working in the soil? Add a bottle of flavored iced tea and a loaf of homemade zucchini bread tied up in a floral bow (who knew eating your veggies could be so tasty?), and you have the perfect gift for that garden lover!

Do you see, craft queens and art-departed friends, alike: Themed gifts can involve as much or as little craftiness as you want. (Who says you can't rely on a prepackaged zucchini bread mix

GIFTS BY THE BOOK

The Bible is full of examples of powerful gift-giving. Remarkably, these examples show that those who give often receive the greater gift—grace and a taste of heaven. Take a look.

- Abraham and Sarah entertained three strangers at Mamre and delighted them with a gift of food—and it was through these recipients that the Lord told Abraham that Sarah would have a son.
- The poor widow of Zarephath shared her last bit of food with a wandering prophet. The widow had been preparing to make bread for herself and her son when Elijah turned up on her doorstep and asked for something to eat. The widow put this stranger in need ahead of herself—and her family. In the end, God rewarded the widow during the long drought that followed, making sure she never ran out of flour or oil to make bread for her family.
- The little lad who supplied two fish and five loaves of bread made possible Jesus' feeding of the five thousand, showing how generosity can result in a greater good for the kingdom of God.

The Greatest Gift

No book on gift-giving would be complete without mention of the greatest gift ever given—and why—from the best-selling book of all time.

"For all have sinned and fall short of the glory of God" (Romans 3:23). The verse says it all. Every person has done things that displease God and fall short of His holy standards.

"For the wages of sin is death, but the gift of God is eternal life through Christ Jesus our Lord" (Romans 6:23). God, in His great love for every person, offers to all the free gift of eternal life!

"For God so loved the world that he gave his one and only Son, that whoever believes in him shall not perish but have eternal life" (John 3:16). Anyone who believes God sent His only Son to die for us—taking the punishment that we deserve—can enjoy this gift.

"For it is by grace you have been saved, through faith—and this not from yourselves, it is the gift of God—not by works, so that no one can boast" (Ephesians 2:8–9). There's nothing anyone can do to earn eternal life—it is a gift with no strings attached.

"I write these things to you who believe in the name of the Son of God so that you may know that you have eternal life" (1 John 5:13). Once the gift is received by faith, there's joy and assurance of eternal life through Jesus Christ.

"Thanks be to God for his indescribable gift!" (2 Corinthians 9:15).

now and then, wrapped your own way with personalized instructions?)

So who else is on your gift list?

- a chocolate lover?
- a barbecue grilling wanna-be?
- a raspberry connoisseur?
- a baseball fanatic?
- a grandpa who loves to fish?

Ideas will begin to flow as you redirect your energy from wandering department store aisles in search of "what to get for this occasion" to "whom do I want to celebrate and what makes them wonderful?"

May words from what we consider one of our greatest gifts—the Bible—motivate you as it does us: "Each one should use whatever gift he has received to serve others, faithfully administering God's grace in its various forms" (1 Peter 4:10). That's what a homespun gift really is—a little grace, like a piece of your heart that you leave behind.

Thinking Outside the (Gift) Box

When it comes to gift-giving, you're sure to have friends and relatives on your lists every season. But are there others? Whom do you cross paths with every week? How might you touch a life with a little something for a silly reason, or no reason at all, just to show you care?

Whether it's the crossing guard at the corner, your barber or hairdresser, the woman who plays piano at church week after week, or the retired gentleman who bags your groceries in a careful manner, there are people all around you who would be surprised—and grateful—to know you care about them.

Karen discovered this when her family moved to St. Johns, Michigan. In this small Midwestern town, the big excitement of the day was the arrival of the mail. Karen and her kids eagerly looked forward to what their postman, Mr. Brown, would bring to their doorstep: letters, flyers, news from the world beyond their front yard. Mr. Brown made every day special just by doing his job with a smile, the kids decided, so why not create one day especially fun for him?

They pooled their change for a gift certificate so Mr. Brown could take Mrs. Brown out for a nice supper to "the best place to eat in town": the Dairy Queen. At the Dollar Store they found a squirt gun, perfect for warding off ill-mannered or pesky dogs along the mail route. Back home, they baked cookies and brewed some iced tea, ready to be poured for quick refreshment on a hot day.

Voila! Mr. Brown Day was about to commence.

As Mr. Brown eased his way around the corner of their walkway the next morning, the kids jumped onto the front steps, blowing party horns and tossing confetti in the air.

"Surprise!" they shouted. "Mr. Brown—best mailman in town! This is officially Mr. Brown Day!"

Mr. Brown smiled, gratefully sipped the tea, and enjoyed the cookies, compliments, and gifts. Then he pocketed the gift certificate, secured the squirt gun to his knapsack, and went on his way.

A few weeks later, Karen was cleaning little fingerprints off the living room picture window when Mr. Brown showed up at his usual time with the daily mail. She went outside to greet him.

"You know," he said, taking off his sunglasses, "I've been a mailman in this town for thirty-three years, and no one has ever done anything like what your family did for me." He shook his head and smiled. "Thank you. I'm still not over Mr. Brown Day."

Neither are Karen's kids. They're itching now to do good, love well, and give gladly.

Imagine—how might some gift from your heart change someone else's life—and yours?

2

BUTTONS AND BOWS,
TINS AND TWINE

· ·

S o you've decided to rise above the humdrum routine of uncreative gift-giving and make each new present as special as the person to receive it. Now what? First, you'll want to establish a well-stocked gift-giving center with some common elements and supplies. Whatever you need to complete your present—whether it's buttons and bows, or tins and twine—you'll want to keep in this convenient center.

If you think that this means you must clear a room or buy a new armoire, take heart! Your gift-giving center can be whatever works with what you have: a corner shelf in the pantry, that deep drawer in the kitchen, a lidded-box in the linen closet or under the bed, or an airtight container in the garage. The first step is just that quick and that easy. The next steps can happen in a few minutes or gradually in the days and weeks to come.

From the Store

Let's face it—to have a well-stocked gift-giving center, you need to make a few purchases. You needn't load up on everything at the start of your homespun mission, though, or buy a long list of supplies at one time and full price. The following items will help you fashion beautiful things with ample supplies that you stock over time by scouting discount stores, postseasonal and clearance sales, and even yard sales and flea markets.

FABRIC

Muslin, holiday prints, pretty plaids, and cheerful chintzes are great when you need a simple gift bag or a quick jar topper for a layered cookie mix. Layer various complementary fabrics for a finished look.

SCISSORS

Those new, decorative-edged scissors are wonderful for cutting out a gift tag, and pinking shears are great for cutting a piece of fabric for lining a basket.

PATTERNS

If you're handy with a sewing machine, be sure to have a couple of standby patterns in your sewing drawer. Great ones to look for are:

- baby booties and teddy bears for quick baby shower gifts
- a tea cozy for a handy hostess gift
- charming embroidery designs—especially letters of the alphabet—for personalized and monogrammed hand, tea, or dish towels
- interesting-shaped pillows or tube pillows for any occasion

BUTTONS

No craft cupboard would be complete without a jar of buttons. Start saving buttons now or look for them in bulk at craft or fabric stores. Lots of buttons glued on in layers can make an old picture frame look new. Use all white buttons on a frame for the photograph of a bride-to-be trying on her wedding dress. String brightly colored buttons on a cord for an interesting necklace or bracelet. For cards, glue a single button in the center, or glue a ribbon off to one side with one large button placed strategically or lots of little ones evenly spaced in a row.

PAPER

Make your own cards and gift tags with any kind of paper. Buy card stock, which comes in a variety of colors and textures, or poster board and construction paper as you find it on sale. Blank index cards work great too; they're almost the same weight as card stock at half the price (but half the color selection too).

The more varieties of colors, designs, textures, and weights of paper that you collect, the greater your chances of sparking something truly imaginative and unique.

Think of the possibilities: You can stamp on paper; cover it with pencil etchings or geometric lines in colored marker; paint it; write on it; photocopy pictures onto it; print your own gift tags; or photocopy any of the gift tags in chapter 10.

You can fold paper like an accordion into a fan or roll it into a cone for a gift container.

Etchings can be made by laying paper on a dimensional surface and rubbing for an impression with a pencil, chalk, or even a crayon.

To do your own embossing, press a piece of paper just enough between two raised surfaces to raise and embed a shape.

White or light-colored tissue paper looks sophisticated atop darker colored paper for gift wrap or an invitation.

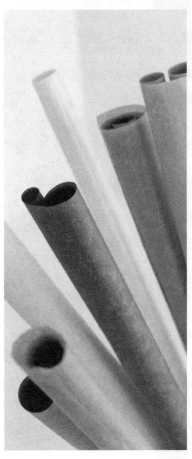

OTHER NECESSITIES

- ribbon of all kinds—satin, silk, paper, raffia, cotton, sheer, velveteen, organza
- jute twine or old-fashioned heavy string and cord
- writing utensils of all kinds from markers and calligraphy pens to colored pencils and gel pens (and never underestimate the elegance of a black pen with fine ink)
- rubber stamps
- inked stamp pads
- tape—double-stick, foil, masking, strapping, white cloth, or any other kind
- acrylic craft paints in assorted colors
- paintbrushes and sponges in all shapes and sizes
- tissue paper of all colors
- paper bags, from lunch-sized sacks to miniatures

Around the House

Usable items are usually close at hand. Look around you right now and you're bound to see something; cruise from room to room and, with a keen eye and some imagination, you'll find even more. For starters:

GREETING CARDS

You can cut up old cards and crop their covers to mount on card stock for your own personalized notes. Colored envelopes work too; cut them into interesting shapes with decorative scissors for a quick tag. Try layering two cards of different patterns and colors on top of each other, making the one on top slightly smaller; punch a hole near the top and fasten together with curling ribbon or a bow. Presto! You've fashioned an elegant invitation, ornament, or wall hanging.

CALENDARS, MAGAZINES, AND CATALOGS

Before you toss away any of these used or viewed items, clip any art or type you could recycle for decorating your own gift cards and tags.

BOXES, CONTAINERS, AND PACKAGES

Some food containers can do double duty—both as packages for gifts, and as gifts themselves. Those plastic hand-wipe containers that snap shut make perfect "treasure boxes," and boxes with lids can be covered with pretty paper to hold flowers, wrapped candy, or other goodies.

Some containers don't even need decorating. For instance:

- Oatmeal canisters (the ones with that handsome elderly gentleman on the front) can hold your oatmeal cookies or muffins. For the top, cut a square of brown paper from a grocery bag with zig-zag-edged scissors and tie with some jute twine for an old-fashioned look.
- Cocoa tins work perfectly for storing your famous homemade fudge or a tasty, hot chocolate mix.
- Seed packets, like those for "forget-me-nots," can hold all sorts of things with an unforgettable printed message.
- Extra drinking glasses that don't match your set can hold homemade cookies for a "cookies and milk" gift.

TIN CANS

Large tin cans (the no. 10 size) or ones used for canned tomato juice can display gifts inventively. Make sure the top is removed and any sharp edges are bent down with pliers, or use the kind of can opener that takes off the top completely, leaving no sharp edges. Cover the can with a coat of nontoxic, acrylic paint, or maybe even a crackle or marbled finish. Glue a painted wooden shape on the side and finish with a raffia bow for a beautiful handmade "gift box."

Another idea is to make lovely homemade lanterns out of any size can. Fill the tin can with water and freeze it. Then, using a hammer and a small, sharp nail, punch a pattern into the sides of the can. You may want to outline your pattern first by drawing onto the tin a succession of dots to be punched. For a hanging lantern, poke a hole in each side of the can at the top and thread a wire through for a handle. Use the lantern to hold another gift or put a votive candle inside.

JARS

Homemade layered mixes are often put in quart canning jars. To make it more cost-efficient, save mayonnaise jars, which have the same capacity as quart canning jars. Many other standard jars come in perfect shapes for reuse too: salsa, jams and jellies, peanut butter, pickles. Look for canning jars at garage and yard sales. You might even set up a box in the church kitchen to collect jars others would ordinarily discard.

CLOTHING

When your boys (why is it always the boys?!) wear a hole through their blue jeans, don't discard the jeans—cut them off and hem them into shorts. Then save the remainder to use as jar toppers. Cut a circle a bit larger than the circumference of the jar and tie on the denim topper with ribbon or twine.

Don't limit yourself to denim, though. Before throwing out any damaged piece of clothing, old sheets, or pillowcases, check to see if there are remnants that might make good jar or box tops. Solids, florals, and plaids work especially well.

Remember, many treasures are made from little scraps.

LACE DOILIES OR HANDKERCHIEFS

Lace doilies look especially pretty placed on top of a jar and secured with pastel ribbon. Handkerchiefs make the perfect gift wrap for smaller items. Simply bring opposite corners together and tie.

DISHCLOTHS AND HAND TOWELS

Fold a new dishcloth into fourths to fit perfectly over the top of a regular-mouth canning jar, and finish off with a tie of twine. Your loved one then has a lovely gift inside the jar plus a bonus—a new rag to wash her dishes!

Kitchen towels can be used to line a basket filled with fresh-baked cookies. Or, fold two towels into squares, lay a package of recipe cards on top, and tie the bundle with jute twine to inspire the creative juices of a friend with culinary talents. For a finishing touch, tie into the bow a lovely handled utensil, wooden spoon, or small rolling pin.

PAPER LUNCH SACKS

Stencil a pretty design onto a lunch sack for a cute gift bag or trace an image on the front of the bag with either a stencil or a cute cookie cutter. Then carefully cut out the shape and line the inside with tissue paper so the contrasting color "pops."

For a stained glass effect, cut shapes in the bag and cover each one by taping from the inside either colored cellophane or foil.

Before throwing a container or bag away, think how you might use it to package some future gift—you'll not only be stocking your supply center, you'll be practicing good stewardship.

AN ODE TO THE BUTTON

As a little girl, Kelly often played with her grandmother's button box. Sometimes she sat alongside her grandmother as they sorted through the different shapes, sizes, and colors for that just-right one. Other times, they played the game "Button, button, who's got the button?" Every moment spent poring over those fabulous squares, disks, and orbs has become a cherished memory.

Think of folks you know who share these same kinds of memories of their grandmothers' button boxes or their mothers' sewing kits.

Buttons not only fasten shirt sleeves to keep people warm, they also conjure up a cozy, homespun feeling by simply popping up on a gift tag or as part of a homespun gift.

3

MARVELOUS MIXES

· ·

raft shows and country shops today have gone crazy with giftable mixes. Layered in jars or tucked in cute cloth bags, these easy-to-fix foodstuffs are everywhere. They're also pricey.

Why not make your own? Not only will you ease the strain on your wallet, you'll save time searching for just the right mix for just the right person.

This chapter includes some of the best tried-and-true mix recipes we've found and developed over the years. They're good for nearly everyone on your gift list: friends, teachers, coworkers, and coaches.

Along with the suggestions for various ways to tastefully package the mixes, you'll also find references to the back of the book for corresponding gift tags that detail "the fixing" instructions. Photocopy the tag on card stock, cut out with decorative scissors, and include it with each gift for the finishing touch.

Hmmm . . . homemade charm, store-bought quality. . . .

If you don't tell about this great gift secret, neither will we!

Soups

BLACK BEAN SOUP

This hearty, thick soup is a meal in itself when served with some crusty, homemade bread! The mix looks homey and heartwarming too when placed in a clear jar topped with black-and-white fabric and tied with white ribbon. Note: One recipe will fit in a pint jar; double the recipe for a quart jar.

Another way to give this mix is to package it in a reclosable plastic bag that you can slip into a brown paper lunch sack trimmed at the top with wavy scissors. Fold the top over and punch two holes about three inches apart to secure with ribbon that's threaded through the holes and tied into a lovely bow.

    2   cups dry black beans
    3   tablespoons dried parsley
    ¼   cup minced, dried onion
    2   teaspoons salt
    2   teaspoons chopped, dried garlic

Place the beans in the chosen container. In a small, reclosable snack bag, mix the remaining ingredients. Place the snack bag on top of the beans and close. Attach a copy of the instructional tag on page 134.

SPLIT PEA SOUP

This soup is a stick-to-your ribs favorite, and it tastes even better the second day after it's made. You can give this mix in a canning jar, a home-sewn bag (see how to make these on p. 129), or even a clear plastic bag tied with green curling ribbon and placed in a terra-cotta pot to give a fresh-from-the-garden feel.

    3   cups split peas
    ½   cup dried lima beans
    ¼   cup pearl barley
    2   tablespoons parsley
    1   tablespoon celery seed
    1   tablespoon onion powder
    2   teaspoons salt

2 teaspoons garlic powder
1 teaspoon dried thyme
1 teaspoon dried basil

Mix all the ingredients and place them in your chosen container; be sure to include the tag on page 134. For attractive layering in a clear jar, place the ingredients in this order:

1. herbs and spices: salt, garlic powder, onion powder, thyme, celery seed, basil, and parsley
2. pearl barley
3. split peas
4. lima beans

CREAM OF POTATO SOUP

If you're looking for a creamy, comforting meal on a cool autumn evening, this is it! Place this mix in a basket with four bowls and four coordinating fabric napkins with napkin rings, and you've got an encouraging gift for a busy family.

1¾ cups instant mashed potatoes
1½ cups dry milk
2 tablespoons chicken bouillon granules
2 teaspoons dried minced onion
1½ teaspoons seasoned salt
1 teaspoon dried parsley
¼ teaspoon pepper

Combine all ingredients in a large bowl and pour into a quart jar. For a cute jar topper, place an eight-inch circle of fabric over the top of the jar. Photocopy the tag with fixing instructions on page 134. Punch a hole in one corner of the tag. Tie a bow with jute twine under the rim of the jar to hold the fabric in place and tie the tag into the bow. For a finishing touch, use a hot glue gun to attach a button onto each end of the twine bow.

FINE DINING IN A POT!

Warm someone with a Soup and Bread Night in a pot. You'll need a large speckled enamelware pot, either a new one to give away, or a cleaned-up one from an antique shop or a yard sale. Line the inside with a dish towel. Fill the pot with a few soup mixes in bags and some handy bread mix in a new bread pan. Add a soup ladle or perhaps a pepper grinder. How about some soup mugs featuring the Campbell's kids, or a new hot pad and oven mitt? Tie some raffia around the pot and secure with double-sided tape. Mmm-mmm, good!

FRENCH MARKET SOUP

Ooh-la-la! This colorful mix makes a beautiful gift to use or display on your kitchen counter. For fun, place this packaged mix in a basket lined with a new dish towel; include a loaf of French bread, a map of France, perhaps a tiny toy Eiffel tower, and a book about the sites you might see if you were to visit Paris or the Provencal countryside. Whoever receives this inspiration is sure to exclaim, *"Merci, merci, mon ami!"*

½ cup each:
　　navy beans
　　pinto beans
　　black beans
　　split peas
　　lima beans
　　kidney beans
　　cranberry beans
　　northern beans
　　or any other combination of dried beans totaling 4 cups

Mix the beans and peas in a large bowl and pour into a quart jar. For an eye-catching presentation, layer them in a clear container or jar and tie a bow (raffia looks lovely) around the top or jar rim. Try tying a small wooden spoon into the bow and don't forget the instructional tag on page 135.

Breads

HANDY BREAD MIX

This mix is great to have on hand to whip up a delicious loaf of homemade swirl bread or pizza dough. Give it to a family who has just moved into your neighborhood.

10 cups bread flour
½ cup sugar
4 teaspoons salt

Mix all the ingredients together and store—or give away—in an airtight container. This mix can be used to make Homemade Pizza, Italian Breadsticks, Apple Cinnamon Swirl Bread, or Chocolate Raspberry Swirl Bread. Look for complete instructions for these recipes on pages 135–137.

FIVE-FRUIT BREAD

Give this mix along with a can of fruit cocktail and some fruit-shaped candies (like jellied orange or lemon slices) in a basket lined with a colorful dish towel.

- 1 cup flour
- 1 teaspoon baking soda
- 1 teaspoon salt
- ⅔ cup white sugar
- ⅓ cup brown sugar
- 2 teaspoons cinnamon
- 3 tablespoons coconut

Place the first four ingredients in a quart-size reclosable bag labeled MIX. Place the brown sugar, cinnamon, and coconut in a sandwich-size reclosable bag labeled TOPPING. Place both bags in a simple cloth pouch sewn from fruit-patterned or calico material. Finish your gift with a copy of the tags on page 138.

CAKELIKE CORN BREAD

Give this mix in a fabric bag with a Western motif. Tie the bag with a length of leather lacing. Couple it in a basket with any of the soup mixes dressed up with a bandanna on top and a leather lacing bow. The corresponding tag is on page 137.

- 1½ cups buttermilk baking mix
- 1 cup cornmeal
- ½ cup sugar
- 1½ teaspoons baking powder

Mix ingredients in a bowl and pour them into a medium-size plastic bag.

THE LANGUAGE OF BREAD

The power of flour, butter or oil, and yeast when mixed, measured, kneaded, and baked can transcend any language, any time. Bread, after all, means life in every culture. Its very essence and aroma not only speak to the stomach but also the soul. The very act of breaking bread is symbolic of sharing—offering community, communion, and friendship; and bread itself is a symbol of generosity and success.

So sharpen your fluency in the language of bread gifts. Include any of the following with every loaf of homemade bread or package of bread mix that you offer to a friend:

- a bread board and knife
- a decorative-handled butter spreader
- a bread warmer
- loaf pans
- a butter mold and flavored butters; mix softened butter with savory herbs (like dill or peppers), sweets (like honey or berries, freshly grated ginger, vanilla and brown sugar, freshly grated nutmeg, or cinnamon), or even nuts (like ground hazelnuts)
- a handmade coupon for one evening of breaking bread together at your place

FRESH STRAWBERRY BREAD

This mix is perfect for whenever berries abound. Offer it as a ready-and-waiting mix for those first and last tastes from the garden. Package the mix in a bag tied with pink or red (or both) ribbon and tucked into a new loaf pan lined with a summery fabric. To make things especially simple, include a quart of fresh berries and the gift tag on page 136.

3	cups flour
2	cups sugar
1¼	teaspoons cinnamon
1	teaspoon baking soda
1	teaspoon salt

Mix the dry ingredients in a large bowl; carefully pour the mixture into a gallon-size plastic bag. Secure the top with a twist tie and decorate with red curling ribbon.

HARVEST PUMPKIN BREAD OR MUFFINS

This versatile recipe can be made into a loaf of delicious bread or twelve tasty muffins. Tags for both recipes are included on page 139. For a jar topper, add a fabric circle (in a harvest color or pattern) on the lid and tie with raffia, twine, or even a dried corn husk.

Mix the following ingredients and put in a quart jar:

1½	cups whole wheat flour
½	cup sugar
2	teaspoons baking powder
¾	teaspoon salt
1	teaspoon ground cinnamon
1	teaspoon ground ginger
½	teaspoon ground cloves
½	teaspoon nutmeg

Add on top of flour mixture, in order:

½	cup golden raisins
½	cup brown raisins
½	cup sunflower seeds

To top things off, mix and place in small snack bag:

2½	teaspoons sugar
1	teaspoon cinnamon

For a unique gift presentation, cut a medium-size pumpkin in half crosswise, so you end up with two bowl shapes. Clean out the bottom bowl and arrange some pretty fall napkins inside. Put the mix on top of the napkins, along with a small can of pumpkin. Talk about a treat!

Muffins

GINGER SPICE MUFFINS

A refreshing fall favorite! Great for families on the run! Place this mix in a quart jar and put twelve decorative fall muffin liners in the top of the jar. Tie a bow around the rim of the jar and glue a dried orange slice to the center of the bow, along with the tag on page 139.

1¾	cups flour
2	tablespoons sugar
1	tablespoon baking powder
½	teaspoon baking soda
½	teaspoon nutmeg
½	teaspoon ground ginger
½	teaspoon ground cloves
½	teaspoon salt
1	cup cinnamon baking chips

Mix all the above ingredients and place in a quart-size canning or mayonnaise jar.

MUCH ADO ABOUT MUFFINS

It doesn't take much to delight someone with a yummy muffin mix or some fresh-baked muffins, but adding any of the following increases the inventiveness of your gift:

- a new muffin tin
- kitchen timer
- wooden spoons
- beautiful pottery mixing bowl
- a box of herbal tea
- cinnamon sticks tied in a bow
- a colorful mug
- flavored butters (mix berries or herbs like mint or fresh-grated ginger into some softened butter and place in a jar or freeze in a mold and give in an airtight plastic container)
- pretty napkins rolled, tied with ribbon sash
- matching tiny bread plates from a discount store or mismatched ones in a favorite color theme from a garage sale or antique shop

29

CHOCOLATE CHIP MUFFINS

The chocolate fan on your list will love this perfect item to round out that chocolate lover's gift basket. Be sure to include some hot cocoa mix, favorite chocolate candy bars, a chocolate-scented candle, and a handful of candy kisses.

2	cups all-purpose flour
2	teaspoons baking powder
½	teaspoon salt
⅓	cup brown sugar
⅓	cup sugar
1⅓	cups milk chocolate chips

Mix the first three ingredients in a small bowl. Pour the mixture into the bottom of a quart canning jar. Layer the brown sugar, then the white sugar, and finally the chocolate chips. You may want to tap down the layers as you go in order to fit them all into the jar. Close the jar and tuck a candy bar into a bow made from curling ribbon. Don't forget the tag on page 140.

COFFEE CAKE MUFFINS

These muffins bring back memories of breakfast in Grandma's kitchen with fresh-baked coffee cake still warm from the oven. Why not give Grandma a taste of what she gave you so many years ago! Slip the two reclosable bags from this mix into one homemade calico bag. Tie a ribbon with a scrap piece of lace, making sure to include the instruction tag on page 140. You could even add a small wooden spoon or a coffee mug for a finishing touch!

In a quart-size reclosable bag mix the following:

1½	cups all-purpose flour
½	cup sugar
2	teaspoons baking powder
½	teaspoon salt
½	cup cinnamon baking chips (optional)

In a snack-size reclosable bag mix the following:

- ¼ cup brown sugar
- ¼ cup chopped walnuts or pecans
- 1 teaspoon cinnamon

LEMON POPPY SEED MUFFINS

These are good standbys and are especially appropriate when a family you know comes down with chicken pox; we call these "Chicken Pox Muffins." You can give the muffins or mix in a basket along with a few lemons and flavored teas. Don't forget the recipe tag on page 140.

- 1 store-bought lemon cake mix
- 3 tablespoons poppy seeds

Mix the two ingredients in a gallon-size reclosable plastic bag. You're done! (Wasn't that easy?)

Cookies and Bars

MICHIGAN DRIED CHERRY-CASHEW BARS

Northern Michigan is famous for its cherries, and you'll discover why when you taste these mouthwatering bars (pictured on the cover) made with the dried fruit. Incidentally, a drop cookie version of this recipe won a Blue Ribbon at the Clinton County Fair in St. Johns, Michigan, in 1998!

- 1½ cups all-purpose flour
- ½ teaspoon baking soda
- ⅓ cup sugar
- ½ cup brown sugar
- ½ cup vanilla chips
- ¾ cup dried tart cherries
- ⅓ cup chopped cashews

In a quart jar, layer the ingredients in the order given. Be sure to tap down the ingredients after every layer in order to get everything into the jar. Don't worry if all the cashews don't fit the jar you use, just add what you can until they reach the top. Don't forget to include the tag with cookie-making instructions on page 141.

PEANUT BUTTER CHIP COOKIES

This simple, satisfying cookie recipe is especially appealing when paired with peanut butter cup candy or a homemade flavored coffee mix. The combination makes a great afternoon pick-me-up.

1¾	cups all-purpose flour
1	teaspoon baking soda
1	teaspoon salt
½	cup cocoa powder
½	cup brown sugar
½	cup sugar
1	cup peanut butter chips

Layer the ingredients in order in a quart jar. Attach the tag on page 142 for instructions.

FAMILY FAVORITE SUGAR COOKIES

Along with giving the dry ingredients and the instructions for these homemade cookies, include some cute seasonal or thematic cookie cutters. Kids and kids-at-heart love making these cookies, which can be decorated in so many ways: with candies, sprinkles, colored sugar, icing, or corn syrup with food coloring that's painted on prior to baking for a stained glass effect.

5	cups all-purpose flour
1	teaspoon baking soda
1	teaspoon cream of tartar

In a large bowl, sift dry ingredients together. Put mixture in a bag and add the tag on page 142.

OATMEAL COCONUT CRUNCHIES

This layered cookie mix might cost you as much as $10 in a country shop, but you can easily whip up several batches for under $1 each by buying the needed items in bulk. Be sure to add a cute topper and the ready-made tag on page 142.

1   cup rolled oats
½   cup coconut
½   cup semi-sweet chocolate chips
¼   cup white baking chips
1⅛ cups flour
½   teaspoon baking soda
1   teaspoon baking powder
¼   teaspoon salt
¾   cup brown sugar

Spoon the brown sugar into a wide-mouth quart jar, pressing down well. Mix the flour, baking soda, baking powder, and salt and place on top of the brown sugar. Then, in this order, layer the rolled oats, coconut, chocolate chips, and white chips.

COWBOY COOKIES

Yee haw! Any buckaroo, young or old, will love these cookies. Pour all ingredients into a gallon-size reclosable bag. Wrap a red bandanna around the bag and secure the bandanna with a length of leather lacing or jute twine. Tie two plastic pony beads to each end of the lacing or twine. Put the mix into a cowboy hat along with a sheriff's badge and a lasso. The Bonanza boys would be proud.

1½   cups all-purpose flour
1   teaspoon baking powder
½   teaspoon baking soda
¼   teaspoon salt
¾   cup brown sugar
½   cup sugar
2   cups rolled oats
2½   cups total any of the following options:
     chocolate chips
     chopped nuts
     raisins or dried fruit
     M&M candies
     coconut

Pour all the ingredients into a gallon-size reclosable bag. Mix thoroughly. Don't forget to lasso the instructional tag from page 143 onto the bag, jar, or container.

Cobblers & Cakes

VERY BERRY COBBLER

This recipe is so simple even the kids can make it on their own. You can make the mix a gift by placing it in a quart-size, reclosable bag; when the recipient's ready to make the cobbler, the batter can be mixed in that same bag. Make sure the bag is tightly sealed before you knead the bag to combine all the ingredients. Don't forget to give a quart of fresh blueberries or raspberries, along with the inspirational label for Proverbs 11:30 on page 149, and the instructional tag on page 143.

    1   cup all-purpose flour
    1   teaspoon baking powder
    1   cup sugar

Put the three ingredients into a quart-size reclosable bag. Seal the bag and mix thoroughly.

CARROT CAKE

This cake mix makes a lovely spring treat! For a birthday, or "Just Because," treat someone special on your gift list to this tasty mix. Place it into a gallon-size reclosable bag and slip into a cloth bag made from a cheerful, spring print fabric. Tie with yellow curling ribbon, making sure to include the instructional tag on page 143. Try pairing this mix with a stuffed rabbit or small, decorative watering can. Or, simply give the mix with three large carrots to use in making the cake!

    2   cups sugar
    ½   cup chopped pecans
    3   cups all-purpose flour
    2   teaspoons baking soda
    1   tablespoon cinnamon
    ¼   teaspoon nutmeg

Blend the dry ingredients together and place in a gallon-size reclosable bag.

APPLE SPICE CAKE

This mix puts a new twist on the old idea of giving an apple to the teacher. Make several batches and give all your children's teachers (school, piano, church) a heartwarming treat at the beginning of the year, at midyear, or at the end of the season.

This mix looks especially cute when placed in a homemade calico pouch (see p. 129). Place your mix ingredients in a gallon-size reclosable bag and slip that into the cloth pouch that you'll tie shut with raffia or other ribbon. Glue on a couple of cinnamon sticks and a dried apple slice for a homey feel. Be sure to include an instructional tag from page 141.

For any occasion, give this in a new mixing bowl or cake pan (why not look for a novelty-shaped one?).

3	cups all-purpose flour
1½	cups sugar
1	teaspoon baking soda
1½	teaspoons cinnamon
½	teaspoon nutmeg
½	teaspoon salt
1	cup chopped pecans or walnuts

In a large bowl, combine all the above ingredients. Place in a gallon-size reclosable bag.

THE LAYERED LOOK!

Jars make the perfect container for storing and presenting many gift mixes—and they can be reused by the recipient. So what about your secret cookie recipe?

It's easy to adapt it, like many of your favorite mix recipes, to fit into a quart jar!

First, look over the needed dry ingredients to make sure they total four cups, give or take a few tablespoons. If you're way over four cups of materials, you'll need a bigger jar.

Next, layer ingredients in the jar, beginning with the powdery dry ones, for instance, flour, baking soda or powder, and salt.

Spoon on the remaining ingredients that are bulkier (and showier), such as oatmeal, sugar, chocolate chips, raisins or other dried fruit, and nuts.

Attach a tag that lists the liquid or fresh ingredients needed to complete the recipe—like eggs, oil, or milk—along with directions for baking.

Look for canning jars on sale just after the garden season or pick up old but still good jars at garage and yard sales. You often can buy lids at Dollar or drug stores. With decorative lids and labels, you can attractively reuse almost any kind of jar.

For more uniquely shaped jars, check out import shops and markets, but be sure to check the size of the jar for capacity as well as the mouth of the jar for how practical it will be for storing and pouring ingredients.

Wedding Announc

4

LET'S LEAVE A LEGACY

. . . .

*W*hat a gift when one person passes down something of significance—sharing not just the object but the story behind it. Karen and her family love to repeat how her husband's paternal grandparents acquired many of their kitchen items during the Depression years. Grandma Ehman, who raised her family in northern Michigan in the 1920s and '30s, said one had to be creative in those days to supply the kitchen. Many of her dishes came from the local movie house, where the owners gave out a different piece of china each week to the patrons in attendance. One week you could get a cereal bowl, the next maybe a cup or saucer. As Grandma Ehman's children saved their money to go to the picture show, they were getting more than just a chance to see the latest stars on the silver screen; they were helping round out their mother's dish collection. The children also gave their mother, piece by piece, a set of silver.

Now Karen is the proud owner of Grandma Ehman's silver, and as she and her children pull out each piece to polish and use for the holidays, they marvel. Wonderful things are built one piece at a time, by everyone working together.

You too can capture your family's legacy (even if it's one in-the-making) to share with your family, whether it's big or small or extends to a close-knit circle of friends. Everyone has a piece of their past to share, and you'll be surprised by the remarkable ways to do so—with heirlooms or copies of them, special recipes, photographs, or meaningful tales.

Picture It

SOMETHING OLD

For a family member who is getting married, photocopy and frame wedding pictures of ancestors in antique-looking collage frames. Below each photo, write in calligraphy the names and wedding dates of each couple as well as the location of each wedding.

HERITAGE IN THE BAG

For a clever gift bag, photocopy a family picture onto transfer paper. Iron the image onto a simple muslin bag. Place your gift inside.

PACKAGE THE FAMILY RECIPES

If you have a family member famous for making a particular food item, help them create their own product line.

For example, if Grandma is well known for her blackberry jam, can a batch of it in the summer when blackberries are plentiful. Then photocopy a photograph of her just large enough to fit on the lid of the jar. Take the ring from the canning jar and trace a circle on the photo, making sure to center the image. Cut out the picture and glue onto the lid. Finally, glue lace around the top of the jar and add a decorative label on the side that says, "Grandma's Blackberry Jam."

For a cookie or bread recipe, glue several photos on a brown paper bag (tied with twine), on a papier-mâché box, or even on a shoe box covered with brown craft paper.

Hey, Paul Newman's not the only person with the know-how for bottling recipes!

BOX YOUR BEST

Celebrate your family's greatest cooks and welcome someone to your family (whether it's a new bride, foster child, or church member) with this "Best Eats in a Box" gift.

Take a papier-mâché box, available in any craft store, and spray paint it a soft, warm color (plum has that aged and "antiqued" feel). One side at a time, place a $^1/_2$ yard panel of lace on the box and lightly spray paint in a gold or metallic color. When finished, lift off the lace and let the box dry. Follow the same process on the box lid.

On the outside of the box, glue several photos of your family cooks, arranged in collage fashion. Don't forget to label the box with the names of the people in the photos.

Place your family's favorite food items, along with the handwritten recipes, inside. You might include "Mom's Peanut Brittle" or "Grandma's Banana Nut Bread." This box will become a treasure that feeds heart, body, and soul.

BABY TALK

Give those parents-to-be something more to talk about—how the new addition to the family sure looks like Mom, Dad, Grandpa, or Grandma! For a baby shower or gift for the new arrival, frame a picture of both parents or grandparents when they were infants. Include one of the inspirational gift tags that celebrates children on page 144.

FUNNY PHOTO GALLERIES

Frame individual pictures of your children eating watermelon or of everyone blowing bubbles at a family get-together. Or copy in black and white a picture of family members from generations past enjoying Thanksgiving dinner or eating birthday cake. How about a picture of everyone at a family picnic? Anything goes!

Something Old & Something New

RECIPES OF LOVE

Look through Grandma's old recipe box and make color copies of all her favorites on card stock for the children and grandchildren. The copies will be especially treasured, showing all the smudges or spills and dog-eared edges from use over the years.

Cut out each copy with deckle-edge or zigzag scissors. Mat and frame one or two recipe cards on colored paper. You could include a picture of Grandma as you remember her best or as a young woman.

For Christmas, place her Christmas cookie (or any cookie) recipe in a shadow box frame with an antique cookie cutter.

CHINA

For a relative's wedding shower gift, pass on an item from Grandma's china cupboard:

- a glass bowl filled with fruit salad
- a vase filled with fresh flowers
- a teapot stuffed with tea bags in the bride-to-be's favorite blend
- a plate filled with some of Grandma's famous tea cookies

Don't forget the inspirational tag for Proverbs 18:22 on page 145.

PRESENTS BY THE PIECE

If you have an heirloom quilt too damaged to use or display, salvage a portion and frame it as a backdrop to a family photo or a Bible verse written in calligraphy (or even in your own hand, which is like giving a piece of yourself). Don't forget the inspirational tag featuring Joshua 24:15 on page 145.

If enough of the quilt can be saved, make a heart-shaped pillow for a ring bearer to carry at a wedding or a stocking for baby's first Christmas.

SOULFUL SCRAPS

When Trish was young, she remembers her grandmother making quilts for every grandchild to receive on their wedding day. Trish looked forward to the day she would receive her own quilt made by Grandmother's hands.

You don't have to be a grandma, have a grandchild, or get married to make or receive such a special quilt:

How about sending a child off to college with the comforts of home—a quilt from favorite baby clothes or old jeans?

Why not give a birthday lap quilt made from your daughter's old dresses or nephew's too-small dress shirts?

Wouldn't Mother's Day or Father's Day seem even more special with a quilt of squares from each family member who has embroidered their own name and message?

As you sew a quilt by machine or hand, pray for the spiritual life of the person who will receive it; ask for them to be wrapped in God's grace.

FROM THE SHIRTS OFF THEIR BACKS

When our friend Betsy's father died, a family member took his flannel shirts and made teddy bears out of them—one for each of the grandchildren. The children love the cuddly bears, and they still remember Grandpa wearing these shirts as he held them on his lap.

There's no need to wait until your grandpa's gone to take advantage of this wonderful idea. Have the grandkids spend the day with Grandpa and help him clean out his closet now—there must be more than one old shirt in there somewhere. Then ask Grandma to help the children make these teddy bears together. What a day of special memories!

STEPPING STONES

Even kids can make cute stepping stones for a gift for Grandma's garden. You'll need cement mix and some small, cardboard pizza boxes, minus the tops.

Line the inside of the boxes with plastic wrap. Mix the cement according to directions on the package and pour the mix into each lined box.

Have each child personalize their own stone by making their handprint or footprint, writing their name with a small stick, or leaving the impressions from several leaves in the semi-set cement.

Once the cement completely sets and dries, peel off the boxes and plastic wrap. Place your stepping stones in the flower garden to enjoy for years to come.

COVERED BY THE WORD

Photocopy pages of Grandma's Bible to use for wrapping small gifts. Look especially for pages where she's made notes in the margins.

A similar idea is to make a collage of photocopies of her handwritten recipes or old letters for meaningful gift wrapping for the family.

SHADOW BOXING

Use a shadow box frame to display a variety of small heirloom objects. An old quilt, linen handkerchief, or piece of velvet makes a lovely backdrop for old jewelry, thimbles, hair combs, or silver. Simply attach items with craft glue. Use pastel material as a background for baby bonnets or booties.

A STITCH IN TIME

Whether they're from your own closet or sales and shops, antique linens make:

- lovely, quick gift wraps
- backgrounds for framed family photos
- framed showpieces in their own right
- meaningful liners for gift baskets filled with baked goods

To create the antique look of yellowing on new linens, use a dye made from household tea: For each yard of fabric (cotton or wool work best), soak material in a brew made from three tea bags in a sink full of very hot water.

The longer you soak the material (overnight, for instance), the darker the stain. For the faintest stain, soak material thirty minutes or so.

The blacker the tea, the darker the stain you'll get. Peppermint tea leaves can leave a stain that's more green, orange spice tea stains more tan from the cinnamon, and herbal teas such as Celestial Seasonings' Zinger teas will leave stains more pinkish in color.

To set the color, rinse material that's been soaked under cold water, wring it dry, and run it through the dryer.

A SPOONFUL OF GRACE

For a collector of antique spoons, tie a spoon inside a bow on the top of a gift box for a finishing touch to your gift wrapping.

CREATIVITY BY THE CUP

An antique teacup makes another great gift or container. You can fill a teacup with scented wax and a wick to make a candle; or place a box of tea inside the cup, wrap the cup in clear cellophane or tulle netting, and tie it at the top with a pretty ribbon. An inspiring devotional book complements either gift.

POSTCARD MEMORIES

Frame old postcards sent home from military service, vacations, or other travels throughout the States or abroad. This makes a great gift for anyone, especially when you include personal notes, mementoes, or cutouts of you from shots snapped along the way.

THEY COULD BE IN PICTURES

How about celebrating Grandpa or Grandma as the star of your family? Catch them on videotape in a film you direct!

On index cards, gather a list of questions from family members, anything from "Tell us about your first kiss" to "How did you come to know the Lord?"

Now catch Grandpa or Grandma in their favorite chair, turn on the camera, and settle back for a nice long visit. Ask everyone's questions from the index cards and be sure to pause long enough for Grandpa or Grandma to fill in with anecdotes.

Even if the whole family has heard a story a thousand times before, hearing it again in years to come—in Grandpa or Grandma's own words—will become a priceless treasure.

JOURNAL EXCHANGE

In an inexpensive journal, write down a list of questions for a parent or grandparent. Give them the journal for Christmas and ask for it, all filled out, for Christmas the next year. The recipient will have an entire year to get next year's Christmas present ready, and you'll give—and receive back—an unforgettable gift.

PRICELESS BEYOND WORDS

Introducing someone to God and His Word could be the greatest gift you ever give. With this mission in mind, a pastor's wife gave her daughter a used Bible on her thirteenth birthday.

That's right: a used Bible.

The mother had bought a new Bible, read through the entire book in one year, and made little "Mom Notes" in the margins. These notes were written especially from mother for daughter about favorite passages, spiritual yearnings, memories of how a biblical truth was learned, or various people who embodied certain attributes of God.

The Bible was given with a Scripture Reading Plan through the daughter's eighteenth birthday. Not only did the daughter receive insights into her mother's heart but a guide for getting into the Word every day until she was on her own.

What better gift could you give to someone in your family than God's Word—and how better to give it than with a testament of your faith, in your own words?

5

SEASONAL SENSATIONS

. . . .

*A*mazing—the same God who causes the strawberries to ripen in summer makes no two snowflakes alike. His artistic touch, stroking every sense, is evident throughout the year and in every life.

He's placed a magnificent sense of such creativity in you too. Tap into it!

Whether the sun over your head shines or the snow falls, these clever gift ideas will help you chase away the winter blahs or beat the summer heat. In the end, the gifts you fashion will cheer a friend and do some good, which is the greatest sensation.

Winter Warm-Ups

When the temperature falls, do your spirits follow? Even if you live in a warm climate, do you suffer from wintertime blues during the blah, post-holidays?

Nothing can warm your spirits quite like cheering someone else's. Instead of biding your time until spring, try some of these pick-me-up ideas that are even better when shared with a friend. Giving is guaranteed to bring cheer.

S'MORE COOKIES

For a taste of summer in the middle of winter, make a batch of these yummy treats. Give these cookies with a mug and some hot cocoa mix for a treat to enjoy in front of a roaring fire.

- 1 7-ounce jar of marshmallow cream
- 24 graham cracker squares
- 3 12-ounce bags of milk chocolate chips

Spread a thick layer of marshmallow cream between two cracker squares, like a sandwich. Over low heat, melt the chocolate chips. Carefully dip the sandwiches in the melted chocolate, making sure all sides are covered. Cool on wax paper. Wrap individually in cellophane and tie with curling ribbon.

CINNAMON SPICED NUTS

Have you ever caught a whiff of those cinnamon almonds while Christmas shopping at the mall? Instead of waiting until your next shopping trip, make these yourself and share them with a friend! Just place some of the cooled nuts in a clear cellophane bag and tie with curling ribbon.

- 1 egg white
- 2 tablespoons water
- 3½ cups mixed nuts
- ¾ cup brown sugar
- 1 teaspoon cinnamon
- ½ teaspoon ground cloves
- ¼ teaspoon ground nutmeg

Beat egg white and water. Stir in nuts until moist. Drain. Combine dry ingredients. Stir in nuts until coated. Put nuts on greased cookie sheet.

Bake at 250 degrees for 30 minutes.

Enjoy!

OLD-FASHIONED OATMEAL COOKIES

Nothing says "Cozy!" like homemade oatmeal cookies still warm from the oven. Try our recipe below or use your own favorite recipe. For a cute packaging idea, place the cookies in an empty Quaker oatmeal canister and cover with the lid. Out of a paper bag, cut a circle a few inches larger than the top of the canister. Crumple up the paper, then smooth it out and tie onto the top with a raffia bow.

1	cup butter
½	cup shortening
1½	cups brown sugar
2	eggs
½	cup milk
1¾	cups flour
2	teaspoons baking powder
1	teaspoon salt
1	teaspoon cinnamon
¼	teaspoon baking soda
3	cups rolled oats
1	cup raisins, dried cherries, butterscotch chips, or cinnamon chips
½	cup chopped nuts (optional)

Cream the butter, shortening, sugar, and eggs together. Stir in milk. Combine the next five ingredients in another bowl. Add to creamed mixture. Finally, stir in the oats, raisins, and nuts. Bake at 400 degrees for 8 minutes on an ungreased cookie sheet. Cool before packaging so the cookies won't stick together.

TOASTY DRINK RECIPES

Flavored hot chocolate and coffee mixes make great gifts because they can be enjoyed throughout the day and can be packaged so inventively. For instance, any hot chocolate recipe can be packaged in an empty cocoa container, and any coffee recipe can be nicely presented in an empty flavored-coffee canister. You can also present your mix in:

- a glass jar
- baggies nestled in a set of mugs or teacups
- a lovely napkin with matching ones tucked inside
- a sealed plastic bag that's rolled up inside a table runner tied with a beautiful ribbon

Chocolate Mint Coffee

½ cup powdered creamer
⅔ cup sugar
½ cup instant coffee
4 tablespoons cocoa powder
4 peppermint hard candies

Place all ingredients in a blender or food processor. Blend until the mixture is a fine powder. Place the mix in your chosen container. Include the tag on page 147.

Orange Cappuccino

½ cup powdered creamer
⅔ cup sugar
½ cup instant coffee
2 orange-flavored hard candies

Place all ingredients in a blender or food processor. Blend until the mixture is a fine powder. Place the mix in your chosen container. Include the tag on page 146.

Mocha Cappuccino

½ cup powdered creamer
⅔ cup sugar
½ cup instant coffee
¼ cup cocoa powder

Place all ingredients in a blender or food processor. Blend until the mixture is a fine powder. Place the mix in your chosen container. Include the tag on page 146.

Cinnamon Cappuccino

½ cup powdered creamer
⅔ cup sugar
½ cup instant coffee
1 teaspoon cinnamon

Place all ingredients in a blender or food processor. Blend until the mixture is a fine powder. Place the mix in your chosen container. Include the tag on page 146.

Rich & Creamy Hot Chocolate

4   cups powdered milk
1   cup cocoa powder
2   cups sugar
    dash of salt

Mix all ingredients together and place in the container of your choice. Include the tag on page 147.

Mexican Hot Chocolate

⅓   cup brown sugar
¾   teaspoon cinnamon
¼   cup cocoa powder
2½ cups powdered milk

Mix all ingredients together. Place the mix in a quart-size reclosable bag. This mix serves you and a friend! Don't forget the tag on page 147.

White Hot Chocolate

1   teaspoon cinnamon
½   cup white chocolate chips

Mix the two ingredients together. Store or give away in an airtight container. Don't forget to include the tag on page 148.

SNOW PAINT

To surprise children who live in snow country, give them a set of Snow Sprays. You can make these with little spray bottles from the Dollar Store filled with water and a few drops of food coloring.

The next time it snows, send the kids out to paint the town . . . or . . . maybe just the front yard. Have mugs of hot chocolate ready to greet your little Rembrandts.

HANDMADE MITTENS

You don't have to knit or be an expert seamstress to make these symbols of generosity (the open hand), service (the helping hand), and lovingkindness (the extended hand in greeting). You don't need to purchase new fabric to make these either—you can use the polar fleece of any sweatshirt or an old wool sweater.

Wash and dry an old 100 percent wool sweater a couple of times until it feels like wool felt. Now you're ready to begin. Trace a mitten shape around your hand loosely; leave lots of room for fingers to move. Add a half-inch all the way around for the seams. Fold the fabric so that the right sides are together and cut out two sets of mittens. Machine stitch a half-inch seam around the outside of each mitten. Turn right-side-out, and you're done!

You can stitch these by hand, if you wish, following the same steps; once turned-out, on the outside of each mitten, a blanket-stitch in a yarn of contrasting color adds charm.

By the way, mittens not only make a great gift on their own but are also cute tied into the ribbon of almost any gift basket. Include the accent tag on page 160: "Though your sins are like scarlet, they shall be white as snow; though they are red as crimson, they shall be like wool" (Isaiah 1:18).

PINECONE FIRE STARTERS

These work great in the fireplace or for the campfire, adding fragrance in a flash. Collect pinecones on any venture into the woods or buy them at craft shops, flower shops, or drugstores during the holidays. Using tongs, carefully dip pinecones into scented wax that's been melted. Before the wax dries, tuck into each pinecone a short length of wicking. Set the wax-covered pinecones on foil or wax paper to dry.

To use, just light the wick on a pinecone and throw in the fireplace to start a fire with a lovely scent.

SNOWMAN KIT

This inventive gift will wow even the coolest friends.

Of course, the hitch is, they will need to add snow. Everything else is portable though, for the minute the flakes begin to fly. You'll need:

- a scarf and mittens
- sticks for arms

- a stocking cap or top hat made from an oatmeal container painted black and set on a pie tin, also painted black
- buttons or pieces of coal for eyes and buttons
- one carrot (real or plastic) for the nose—and maybe a few others for "nose job choices" and snacking
- a corncob pipe

Place all these items in a box that's been painted royal blue and decorated with white snowflakes. You can stencil on the snowflakes, paint them freehand, or glue on doilies and paper snowflakes made by folding and cutting out shapes along the folds.

Put a label on the box that says "Ye Olde Snowman in a Box Kit" (p. 149) and inspire recipients to keep it for an annual activity.

For an extra treat, include a batch of cocoa mixes and the "Happy Winter" tag on page 148.

THE BOUNTIFUL SNOW BLOCK

For your favorite child (or kid at heart), purchase a snow block mold from a toy store this winter. Turn it upside down to make a basket of sorts and fill it with:

- a pair of mittens
- earmuffs
- a warm hat
- a Frosty the Snowman coloring book
- a box of Crayons
- donuts and packets of hot cider mix

Wrap the mold with cellophane and secure with a bow. Who says snowy weather has to be so frightful?

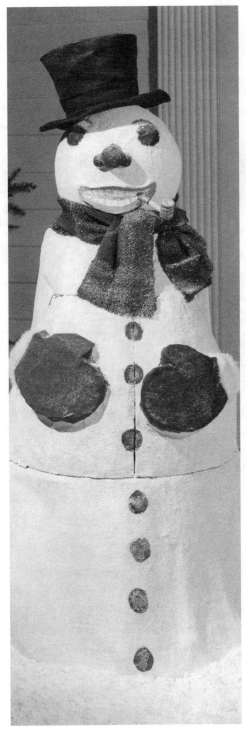

WINTER WHITE FOR WOMEN

You'll have as much fun putting this gift together as the person who receives it will enjoy what's inside. So make your mission "White Night" and fill a basket with anything that's white:

- a fluffy towel
- candles
- milky bubble bath
- White Hot Chocolate mix (see p. 49) nestled in a white mug
- a batch of Macadamia Nut Cookies
- bleached cotton pillowcases
- cotton or woolen slippers

For the perfect finishing touch, don't forget the inspirational gift tag, featuring Psalm 51:7, on page 149: "Wash me, and I will be whiter than snow."

Macadamia Nut Cookies

1¼	cups sugar
½	cup macadamia nuts, coarsely chopped
1	cup white chocolate chips
2	cups all-purpose flour
½	teaspoon baking soda
½	teaspoon baking powder
½	cup butter
1	egg, beaten
1	teaspoon vanilla

Combine the first six ingredients in a medium bowl. In a large bowl, cream the butter with the egg and vanilla. Stir in the flour mixture. Shape into one-inch balls and place on greased cookie sheet. Bake at 375 degrees for 13 minutes.

MOM'S DAY OFF

A great way to give a busy mom a pick-me-up from the winter blues is to pamper her with a day off. First mail her a copy of the certificate on page 150. This entitles her to one day all to herself. Of course, you provide the child care and some extras. Next, the day this mom drops off her children (or you pick them up), give her a basket filled with goodies such as:

- bubble bath
- bon bons or her favorite treat
- a video certificate for her to pick up her favorite classic or new release
- pretty stationery for her to write a letter to a friend or family member
- a box lunch
- a timeless inspirational novel about a woman of passion and purpose, for instance *Christy* by Catherine Marshall
- selected Scripture verses

Sunny Delights

Ah, summertime! How wonderful to run barefoot in the sand, sip lemonade on the porch, throw burgers on the grill, and enjoy the company of friends and neighbors. Summer affords so many good things, including unique opportunities to extend hospitality to those you might not see during the cold winter months.

When you want to make someone else's day a little brighter, check out these cool ideas.

MIXES & MARINADES

These make perfect gifts for anyone, especially a hostess or a new neighbor. Pool your resources with a friend, each of you bringing ingredients for several batches of a few recipes. Mix and match together, so each of you can go home at the end of the day with several different gift mixes and

marinades to keep on hand. Imagine: A package of Ranch Dip Mix and fresh vegetables for the family reunion or a batch of Lemon Pepper Seasoning Mix to take to a friend's house for an impromptu barbecue. You'll always be ready to take advantage of the warm weather and spend time with those you love.

Italian Marinade

This flavorful marinade is simple, healthy to eat, and perfect for the person who loves to grill everything from chicken and beef to fish or vegetables.

¼	cup dried oregano
½	cup dried sweet basil
¼	cup dried minced onion
¼	cup garlic powder
1	tablespoon black pepper
1	tablespoon salt

Mix all ingredients and divide into several small plastic snack bags. Be sure to attach a copy of the instructional tag on page 151.

Cajun Seasoning Mix

This spicy mixture works best on chicken or steak that you grill or broil.

2½	tablespoons paprika
2	tablespoons garlic powder
1	tablespoon salt
1	tablespoon onion powder
1	tablespoon dried oregano
1	tablespoon dried thyme
2	teaspoons cayenne pepper
2	teaspoons black pepper

Mix all ingredients and place in two snack-size reclosable bags. Be sure to include the instructional tag on page 151.

Lemon Pepper Seasoning Mix

Especially good on chicken, the lemon zest adds zip to the meat before you even turn on the heat.

- 1 cup black pepper
- ⅓ cup dried lemon peel
- 3 tablespoons coriander seeds
- ¼ cup dried minced onion
- ¼ cup dried thyme

Mix all ingredients and place in small snack bags. Don't forget the instructional tag on page 151.

Tasty Chicken Coating Mix

- 2 cups dry bread crumbs
- ¼ cup flour
- 3 tablespoons paprika
- 1 tablespoon salt
- 2 teaspoons sugar
- 2 teaspoons onion powder
- 2 teaspoons dried oregano
- 1 teaspoon red pepper
- 1 teaspoon garlic powder
- ¼ cup vegetable shortening

Mix all the dry ingredients together. Cut in shortening until the mixture is crumbly. Place in two pint jars and label with the instructional tag for oven fried chicken on page 152. Be sure to encourage use within six months of receipt.

Southwestern Veggie Dip

- ½ cup dried parsley
- ⅓ cup dried minced onion
- ⅓ cup chili powder
- ¼ cup chopped chives
- ¼ cup ground cumin
- ¼ cup salt

Mix all ingredients and place in small snack bags or half-pint jars. Include the instructional tag on page 153.

Country Dill Dip

Next time you're invited to a casual get-together, offer to bring the veggies and surprise your hostess with a gift of this mix to use on her own later, plus a batch you whipped up for taste-testing now.

    2   tablespoons dill weed
    2   tablespoons onion flakes
    2   tablespoons seasoning salt
    2   tablespoons parsley flakes

Mix all ingredients and place in a small snack bag. Don't forget the instructional tag on page 152.

Creamy Ranch Dressing or Dip

    1½   tablespoons dried parsley
     1   tablespoon salt
     ½   tablespoon lemon pepper
     ½   tablespoon garlic powder
     ½   tablespoon chopped chives
     1   teaspoon dried tarragon
     1   teaspoon dried oregano

Mix all ingredients and place in a small snack bag. Be sure to attach the instructional tag on page 153.

Calico Baked Beans

We get many requests for this dish—a summertime favorite. Present it in a basket lined with red-and-white-checked material, some decorative picnic plates and napkins, and a container of lemonade. Tailgate picnic, anyone?

Place the following in a quart-size reclosable bag:

    1   cup dried northern beans
    ½   cup dried pinto beans
    ½   cup dried red beans
    ¼   cup dried lima beans

In another quart-size reclosable bag, place the following:

- 1 cup brown sugar
- 2 tablespoons garlic powder
- 2 tablespoons onion powder
- 1 teaspoon salt
- ½ teaspoon ground ginger

Fold the two bags together and tie with raffia, making sure to include the tag on page 154.

Mother-in-Law Refrigerator Pickles

These pickles are so delicious, even your mother-in-law will love them. What she doesn't know is how easy they are to make, but why tell her?

- 6 cups pickling cucumbers, thinly sliced
- 2 onions, sliced
- 2 red peppers, sliced
- 3 cups white vinegar
- 2 cups sugar
- 1 teaspoon salt
- 1½ teaspoons mustard seed
- 1 teaspoon celery seed
- ½ teaspoon turmeric

Layer the cucumbers, onions, and red peppers in a large bowl. Combine remaining ingredients in a saucepan. Bring to a boil and cook for 1 minute. Pour over cucumbers. Let cool. Cover and marinate in refrigerator for 2 days. Fill 6 pint jars with mixture. Store in refrigerator. Don't forget the tag on page 154.

Blueberry Marmalade

This jam gives you the flavor of fresh blueberries, even if they're not in season; this recipe will fill 3 pint jars to share with friends. After making a batch of marmalade, and once the jars have cooled, cover each lid with a 7-inch circle of denim and tie with twine.

4	cups crushed blueberries
5	cups sugar
1	lemon
1	orange
¾	cup water
⅛	teaspoon baking soda
6	ounces liquid pectin
⅛	teaspoon ground cloves

Have clean jars waiting in hot water and lids and rings simmering in a saucepan on low heat. Finely grate zests of lemon and orange. Peel, seed, and finely chop the fruits. In a small saucepan, boil zest in water and soda for 5 minutes. Cool. Combine blueberries, sugar, fruit, and the zest mixture in a large saucepan. Bring to a rolling boil. Reduce heat and simmer 10 minutes. Add cloves and liquid pectin. Return to a rolling boil, stirring constantly. Boil 1 minute. Remove from the heat and ladle into clean, hot jars. Adjust lids and rings, screwing down tightly but not over-tightening. Process for 10 minutes in a boiling water bath. Remove jars from the canner and let cool at room temperature for 24 hours. Decorate and add the corresponding gift tag on page 155.

Strawberry Banana Jam

For the person you know who loves strawberries, offer this tasty idea—the next best thing to berries right from the garden. Line a basket with a strawberry-print fabric, then put this jam in along with Fresh Strawberry Bread Mix from page 28, Strawberry Lemonade from page 60, and anything else you can find that fits the theme (strawberry plants, soap, lip gloss, room fragrance—the list is as long as your imagination).

3½   cups crushed strawberries
1½   cups mashed bananas
6¾   cups sugar
3   tablespoons lemon juice
1   box pectin
½   teaspoon butter

Have clean jars waiting in hot water and lids and rings simmering in a saucepan on low heat. Measure fruit and lemon juice into a large saucepan. Measure sugar into a separate bowl. Stir pectin into fruit. Add butter. Bring to a rolling boil, stirring constantly. Quickly stir in all sugar. Return to rolling boil and boil for 1 minute. Remove from heat and skim off any foam. Ladle into hot jars. Adjust lids and rings, screwing down firmly. Process 10 minutes in a hot water bath. Let cool 24 hours. Add the gift tag on page 155.

Spiced Peach Jam

This jam full of sun-ripened flavor makes the perfect complement to a gift of pound cake and some peach-flavored tea bags in a basket lined with a tea towel. The decorative gift tag is on page 156.

4   cups chopped peaches
2   tablespoons fresh lemon juice
5   cups sugar
2   teaspoons ground cinnamon
1   teaspoon ground nutmeg
½   teaspoon ground allspice
½   teaspoon ground cloves
1   box fruit pectin

Have clean jars waiting in hot water and lids and rings simmering in a saucepan on low heat. Measure fruit into a 6-quart saucepan. Add lemon juice and spices. Measure sugar into a separate bowl and set aside. Stir pectin into fruit mixture. Bring to a full boil over medium-high heat. Add sugar. Return to a boil. Boil hard 1 minute. Remove from heat. Carefully ladle into hot jars. Adjust lids and rings, screwing down firmly but not overtightening. Process 10 minutes in a hot water bath. Remove jars from canner and let cool at room temperature for 24 hours. Makes 3 pints.

Strawberry Lemonade

This recipe and the next will quench any thirst during the heat of summer. Why not purchase one of those decorative plastic or glass sun tea jars (with or without a spigot) and give with a batch of this pretty pink lemonade already prepared? Tie a raffia bow around the top of the jar, include the decorative tag on page 156, and bring some plastic cups. Ahhh! That hits the spot.

3	cups cold water		1	cup lemon juice
1	quart fresh strawberries		2	cups chilled club soda
¾	cup sugar			lemon slices

Place water, strawberries, and sugar in a blender. Cover and blend until smooth. If you like, use a fine strainer to remove the seeds in the mixture. Stir in lemon juice and club soda. (You may need to use a large pitcher, if your blender won't hold all the liquid.) Pour into a serving container and add ice and lemon slices.

Raspberry Lemonade

Don't forget the decorative tag on page 157 for this tasty lemonade.

2   packages (10 ounces each) sweetened raspberries, partially thawed
2   cans (12 ounces each) frozen lemonade concentrate, thawed and undiluted
3   tablespoons sugar
2   liters club soda, chilled

In a blender, combine the lemonade, raspberries, and sugar. Strain the mixture using a fine strainer to remove the seeds. Mix the juice with the club soda. You will probably need to use a large bowl or container. Add some ice cubes to chill. Enjoy with friends!

Raspberry Mint Tea

This tea recipe can help cool someone's day. Fill a new thermos with it or present it in an antique 2-quart jar with a lid. Place your container in a small box painted pink and stenciled with green leaves; you could include a small potted mint plant. Add some wrapped raspberry candies to complete your gift and don't forget the tag on page 157.

    4   herbal mint tea bags, steeped in 3 cups boiling water
    1   can frozen raspberry juice concentrate
    1   cup sugar
  3–5 cups water (to taste)

Remove tea bags from water. Add rest of ingredients and mix well. Serve over lots of ice. Refreshing.

Meltless Pops

When the temperature soars, the little ones in your life can enjoy a yummy treat on a stick without a huge, dripping mess. A neighbor or friend who has children around all summer will greatly appreciate a plate of these.

    1   10-ounce bag mini-marshmallows
    ¼   cup butter
    6   cups crisp rice cereal
        Any of these assorted garnishes:

- candy sprinkles
- chopped nuts
- shredded coconut
- milk chocolate chips, melted
- white chocolate chips, melted
- peanut butter chips, melted
- butterscotch chips, melted

Popsicle sticks

In a large saucepan over low heat, melt the butter and marshmallows. Remove from heat and gently stir in cereal. With buttered hands, make balls any size you desire. Push a Popsicle stick into them. Work fast; these set up quickly. Place each pop, with the stick up and the bottom of the ball down, on wax paper. Dip the bottoms of the balls into melted chips and roll them in sprinkles or nuts. Experiment and enjoy!

Ice Cream to Go

Making homemade ice cream is inexpensive enough to let all the neighborhood kids participate—and enjoy. Try this at a block party or family reunion, and you'll make a memory plus be the talk of the town. For each child, you'll need:

½	cup whole milk
¼	cup whipping cream
1	tablespoon sugar
½	teaspoon vanilla extract
1	quart-size reclosable bag
1	gallon-size reclosable bag
2	cups ice
1	tablespoon coarse or rock salt

Carefully pour the milk, whipping cream, sugar, and vanilla into the quart-size bag. Seal tightly, removing excess air. Place ice and salt in the gallon-size bag. Place the sealed quart-size bag inside the gallon bag with the ice and salt.

Now let the kids go wild as they shake, turn, and toss the bags.

Within 15 minutes of shaking and kneading the bags, soft ice cream will begin to form in the smaller bag. Remove the smaller bag, transfer the ice cream to a bowl, or grab a spoon and eat right from the bag. Yummy fun!

HOMEMADE BUBBLES

A few bubbles make for fun, but a bucket? It's a party! This is a great recipe that makes wonderful bubbles and creates hours of play.

Save plastic gallon ice-cream tubs to mix and store the bubbles in a handy container. To decorate the bucket, cut out a piece of colorful, adhesive-backed paper and cover the lid. Then use permanent markers to write words like BUBBLES, BLOW, POP, SUMMER, and FUN on the sides of the bucket in a variety of colors or use the labels on pages 158–159. To personalize, on top of the lid write the child's name, "Jonathan's Bubbles."

12	cups cold water
1	cup Dawn or Joy dishwashing liquid
1	tablespoon glycerin (found in drugstores)

Mix all ingredients together in the bucket. You could also include some common bubble makers found around the house: funnels, straws, plastic carriers from 6- or 8-pack bottles or cans. If these things aren't handy, you can always purchase a set of bubble makers from the store. Store these in a plastic mesh bag to keep everything together.

SIDEWALK CHALK

Here is an activity you can employ on one of those "I'm bored!" days. All children (and many adults!) love to write with chalk on the sidewalk and driveway. This is especially fun for a special friend's birthday. Give a set of chalk as a party favor and have everyone write greetings on the garage pad or sidewalk before they leave the party.

1	cup plaster of paris
½	cup cool water
	liquid tempera paint
	large margarine tubs and sticks for stirring
	molds—Dixie cups, plastic manicotti trays, or toilet paper rolls covered on one end with aluminum foil
	food coloring (your choice)

Put the plaster in the tub, and stir in the water. Add 3 tablespoons of liquid tempera. Mix well. Pour into the molds and let dry completely.

This recipe makes wonderful colors and costs less per stick than store-bought sidewalk chalk. You can make several batches using different colors. To give as a gift, decorate an ice-cream bucket similar to the one for Homemade Bubbles—the handle is great for little hands to carry. Use the label on page 161.

BEACH BASKET FUN

Load up a large basket with everything you need for a day at the beach and invite a family from your church or neighborhood to go along. All they'll need to bring is their swimsuits!

Fold a red-and-white-checked tablecloth and put in the bottom of a basket. Add paper plates, cups, napkins, and silverware. Or purchase discount Frisbees for each child to use for plates, and when they're through eating, they have a handy game! Be sure to include:

- tortilla wrap sandwiches
- apples
- chips
- Meltless Pops (see p. 61)
- watermelon
- cool drinks (bring a jug of cool water with a few fresh lemon slices—refreshing!)
- horseshoes
- a beach ball
- towels
- wet wipes
- sunscreen
- sunglasses

SPARKLER SUNDAES

Place cans of store-bought blueberry and cherry pie filling along with a jar of marshmallow cream in a red, white, or blue basket. Include a half gallon of vanilla ice cream, a box of sparklers for the kids, a small American flag, an ice-cream scoop, and a copy of the book *The 4th of July Story* by Alice Dagliesh to make a patriotic gift for the Fourth of July.

Give this to friends or invite them to share dessert and sparklers with you before the fireworks begin! Don't forget the tag on page 160.

FRUIT OF THE SPIRIT BASKET

How's this for a simple yet encouraging gift for a friend? Place a variety of fruits—apples, pears, grapes, oranges, and bananas in a small basket. Be creative and use whatever's in season. Tie on a floral ribbon bow and, with a small piece of thin floral wire, attach the decorative gift tag on page 161, featuring Galatians 5:22-23. Talk about kindness!

6

BOOKS, BASKETS, AND BUNDLES

. . . .

*I*t's Father's Day. Again. Or your sister's birthday . . . for the thirty-fifth time since you can remember. Never mind that she may thank you for thinking it's only her thirty-fifth birthday—what can you do that feels surprising and wonderful?

This chapter is chock-full of ideas for creating customized baskets and bundles, some built around great works of literature. As you browse through the ideas, put on your thinking caps, because the possibilities here are endless!

The Reader's Nook

When a child's birthday arrives, do you truck off to the store to buy another toy or gadget that may get broken and end up in the trash?

A solution is to give children great literature that, unlike toys, will never grow old. Books can take them to exotic places without ever having to leave home and introduce them to interesting characters without their ever having to shake a hand.

Baskets and bundles centered around the theme of a book will delight children of all ages if you choose the elements carefully, keeping in mind the reading level and genre of books most enjoyed. For winners every time, select classic literature that has stood the test of time. Keep in mind that the youngest of book-lovers—toddlers and preschoolers—especially love colorful board books and read-to-me picture books. Older children love storybooks.

There's no need to always pay full price for books. When you see a great book on sale, pick it up. Don't forget garage and library sales either. You can find practically new items for just pennies. (Remember, although it's nice to borrow books from the library, children need to own their own books and develop a collection that they have access to every day. In time they will learn to cherish books!)

Add the books you find to your gift-giving pantry! Once you choose the right book(s) for the right people, include items that go along with that theme (blank tags are available in chapter 10 for anything you adapt). The ideas that follow are some of our favorites to get you started.

Little House in the Big Woods by Laura Ingalls Wilder illustrated by Garth Williams
Christmas in the Big Woods (My First Little House Books), illustrated by Renee Graef

The Little House books have been loved for so many generations; who can forget how Laura describes what Christmas meant to her as a young child? You could choose the chapter book for the older child or the picture book for someone younger. Title your basket "Laura's Christmas" (use a blank accent tag from chapter 10). Include the items that Laura received that Christmas:

- a red and white striped peppermint stick
- red mittens
- heart-shaped sugar cookie sprinkled with white sugar
- a shiny new penny
- a rag doll named Charlotte
- a tin cup

Winnie the Pooh or *The House at Pooh Corner* by A. A. Milne
A Bear Called Paddington by Michael Bond

Many children are so used to watching the Disney version of Pooh that they never truly meet the original, lovable Pooh! These books are wonderful and should be in every child's home library. Paddington is also a charming bear that children should get to know. These are classics that no child should miss out on! Items to include with one of these books:

- a teddy bear, Pooh bear, or Paddington bear
- honey (in a purchased bear container)
- a couple of boxes of purchased biscuit mix
- a bag of Bit-O-Honey candy

The Pumpkin Patch Parable by Liz Curtis Higgs

Any of the children's books by author Liz Curtis Higgs are wonderful for thematic gift-giving! Give this one with:

- a pumpkin
- a carving knife
- a candle (for inside the pumpkin)
- a jug of apple cider
- a half-dozen donuts

The Parable of the Lily
by Liz Curtis Higgs

During the Easter season, give this book with:

- a lily bulb
- a garden trowel
- gardening gloves

The Parable of the Sunflower
by Liz Curtis Higgs

This story of a young boy who longs to grow sunflowers that reach all the way to heaven will inspire your little one to grow a garden and grow in God's love.

- a packet of sunflower seeds
- a garden trowel
- gardening gloves

The Parable of the Pine Tree
by Liz Curtis Higgs

Give this book to a child who has a December birthday. He or she won't feel forgotten this year! Include:

- a small, potted pine tree to plant in the spring
- hot chocolate mix (see p. 49)
- a box of bright Christmas ornaments

How to Make an Apple Pie and See the World
by Marjorie Priceman

This is a fall-time favorite—both the apple pie and the story, where making an apple pie requires a trip around the world to gather the needed ingredients. Priceman's tale is great for sparking one's imagination and teaching a geography lesson at the same time! Give the book with:

- 6 to 8 Granny Smith apples

- one small jar of cinnamon
- sugar in a small bag
- a pie tin or plate
- a ceramic pie server
- dry ingredients for a pie crust, either from scratch or a mix or a ready-made, refrigerated or frozen pie crust

Two other fall-time favorite apple stories are *3 in 1, A Picture of God* by Joanne Markhausen, which uses an apple to explain to young children the concept of the Trinity; and *Johnny Appleseed* by Madeline Olsen—the legend of that famous American who spreads seeds for everyone to enjoy the taste of apples one day.

What Really Happened to the Dinosaurs by John Morris and Ken Ham

Children will love following Tracker John and his playful little dinosaur friend, D.J., as they explore the world before Noah's flood. Include some fun items to go along with this book:

- a dinosaur play set
- a dinosaur place mat
- dinosaur cookie cutters for cookies or play dough
- a dinosaur coloring book with crayons

Note: To locate other children's materials from a creationist viewpoint, contact The Institute for Creation Research, P.O. Box 2667, El Cajon, CA 92021; or check out their web site (www.icr.org).

The Curious George books by H. A. Rey

Between the three of us we have six boys, and these timeless tales of the curious little monkey named George and his friend, the man with the yellow hat, have always been a hit! Give one book or many along with:

- a stuffed monkey
- a bunch of bananas
- some Monkey Bread and Banana Butter (recipes below)

MONKEY BREAD

2	cans regular-size refrigerator biscuits
½	cup brown sugar
¾	cup white sugar
1	teaspoon cinnamon
½	cup melted butter

Mix the sugars and cinnamon. Cut each biscuit into four pieces and roll each piece in the butter, then the sugar mixture. Layer in a large loaf pan or 9-inch square pan that's been lightly greased. Pour any remaining butter over the top. Bake at 350 degrees for 25 to 30 minutes or until golden brown. Cool and pull apart and eat it with your hands, just like a monkey!

BANANA BUTTER

This makes a tasty treat on a toasted bagel or English muffin. Spread it on pancakes or French toast, or pair with peanut butter for a sandwich sure to please any little monkey.

4	cups mashed, ripe bananas	6	cups sugar
½	cup lemon juice	1	box fruit pectin
1	teaspoon Fruit Fresh (optional)	½	cup butter

Have canning jars in hot water. Simmer rings and lids on low in a small saucepan. In a large saucepan, bring bananas, juice, pectin, butter, and Fruit Fresh to a boil. Quickly stir in sugar. Boil hard for 1 minute. Remove from heat. Ladle into jars. Secure lids and rings. Process 10 minutes in a boiling water bath. Makes 4 pints or 8 one-cup jars.

Math Skill Books

The M&M Counting Book
The Cheerios Counting Book
The Goldfish Cracker Counting Book
The Hershey's Chocolate Bar Fractions Counting Book

These books provide a clever way to sneak in some math skills for the kids! Just package them with the featured item and get ready, set, go!

A Bargain for Frances by Russell Hoban

Any girl will be charmed by the delightful Frances, whose friend, Thelma, badgers her into buying an old plastic tea set. When Thelma says there are no "backsies," Frances comes up with a plan that changes her friend's mind. Just think of all the fun items you could include with this book for some tea parties of your own:

- a children's tea set
- lace doilies
- white linen napkins
- a pretty hair bow or barrette for the tea party
- children's tea (inquire about the ones made by Davidson's, Inc., at any tea or coffee specialty shop)
- tea party invitations

Pancakes, Pancakes by Eric Carle
If You Give a Pig a Pancake
by Laura Numeroff

Kids will love waking up to one of these books with breakfast! Place some pancake mix in a reclosable bag. Slip this into a small lunch sack that has been decorated with stamps or stickers and tied with jute twine. Put the book, the sack, and the following items in a basket:

- a pancake turner
- a bottle of maple syrup
- a quart of blueberries for blueberry pancakes

The Very Hungry Caterpillar by Eric Carle

A hungry critter eats its way through a variety of fruit. Give a copy of the book in a basket full of the fruits he devours:

- an apple
- a pear
- a plum
- a strawberry
- an orange
- a lollipop

The Very Lonely Firefly by Eric Carle

A lonely firefly goes out in search of friends in this wonderful summer bedtime story. Present it with:

- a mayonnaise jar with holes poked in the lid for catching fireflies
- a flashlight
- a bag of marshmallows to roast over a fire

Charlotte's Web by E. B. White

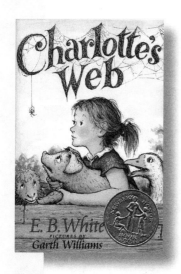

A pig's life is saved by the clever antics of his spider friend in this classic book that displays an important character trait—selflessness. Present this with (you guessed it):

SPIDER COOKIES

2½	cups semi-sweet chocolate chips
¼	cup milk
½	cup peanuts
¾	cup chow mein noodles

In a small saucepan, heat the chocolate chips and milk until chocolate is melted. Stir in peanuts and chow mein noodles. Drop a teaspoonful of batter at a time onto wax paper. Stick in chocolate-covered chow mein noodles for "spider legs." Cool and allow to set before packaging.

Step-Up Biographies or Childhood of Famous Americans Series

Meet George Washington by Joan Heilboner
Meet Abraham Lincoln by Barbara Cary
George Washington: Young Leader by Augusta Stevenson
Tom Jefferson: Third President of the United States by Helen Albee Monsell

Give any of these great books about the founding fathers of our country with a Tin Can Lantern (see p. 19). Line the lantern with patriotic fabric and place a book inside. Add any of the following for an educational and fun book bundle:

- president flash cards
- a United States flag
- play money
- a poster of the presidents
- a "Presidents of the United States" place mat
- stickers

- pencils
- a slate and chalk
- a copy of the Gettysburg Address
- a copy of the Declaration of Independence (roll up and tie!)
- homemade star sugar cookies frosted in red, white, and blue

White Fang by Jack London

This book will take you to a faraway place—Yukon Gold Territory! Animal lovers especially will love the tale of an animal that's part wolf and part dog and of the journey that finally leads him to a gentle master. Place this book in a basket along with:

- Black Bean Soup Mix (see p. 24, and include the tag on p. 134)
- Cakelike Corn Bread Mix (see p. 27, and include the tag on p. 137)
- half gallon of Yukon Gold ice cream

For a younger adventure lover, just beginning to read for himself, build this basket around the early reader with *The Bravest Dog Ever: The True Story of Balto* by Natalie Standford. A brave Balto forges through a terrible snowstorm to bring medicine to the desperate citizens of Nome, Alaska. Based on a true story.

Black Beauty by Anna Sewell
Billy and Blaze by C. W. Anderson

Either book will delight a horse lover. In *Black Beauty,* a horse tells the story of his life, through many different places and masters. In Anderson's tale, Billy loves horses more than anything and receives a pony of his very own for his birthday! Be sure to package along with these books:

- fresh apples or carrots (or apple or carrot chips from the health food or snack sections of your grocery store)
- a gift certificate to a riding stable
- sugar cubes

Old Yeller by Fred Gipson

A stray dog wriggles its way into the heart of a frontier family. Pair this great work of literature in a new dog dish with the following:

- any of the many great film versions of *Old Yelle*r on video
- sugar cookies in the shape of dog bones (recipe on p. 32)
- homemade dog treats (recipe below and tag on p. 162)
- People Chow for the master (recipe on p. 77 and tag on p. 163)

HOMEMADE DOG TREATS

Nothing's too good for man's best friend, including this gift from the heart that you can whip up faster than your canine pal can chase his tail. Use the label on page 162.

3 cups oatmeal	½ teaspoon garlic powder
2 cups whole wheat flour	1⅓ cups water
¼ cup wheat germ	½ cup peanut butter
¼ cup dry milk powder	1 egg

Mix the first five ingredients in a large bowl. In another bowl, blend the water, peanut butter, and egg. Pour the egg mixture into the dry ingredients and stir until blended.

This dough will be stiff as you pat it out to a half-inch thickness. Cut out these dog cookies with cookie cutters.

Bake at 275 degrees for 1½ hours.

Any pup will beg for more.

PEOPLE CHOW

½ cup butter
1 cup peanut butter
2 cups milk chocolate chips

9 cups rice squares cereal
1 pound box of powdered sugar

Melt butter, peanut butter, and chips over low heat. In a large bowl, mix cereal and melted mixture until cereal is well coated. Place powdered sugar in a large paper bag. Pour in cereal and shake until cereal is thoroughly coated.

ANY EARLY READER OR OLD-FASHIONED PRIMER

For anyone just learning to read, give an old-fashioned primer or an early reader book like *Growing Alphabet Soup* by Lois Ehlert—a wonderful story on the basics of gardening with beautiful illustrations. Sparking a new reader's excitement for books now will be a gift in and of itself—the gift of a lifelong love of learning! Including the following will be like icing on the cake—er, alphabet letters in the soup:

- an apple
- A-B-C cookie cutters
- A-B-C or 1-2-3 cookies
- a package of Ready-Reader Alphabet Soup Mix (recipe below)

- a "See Dick and Jane" calendar
- an old-fashioned brass bell
- a chalkboard and chalk

READY-READER ALPHABET SOUP MIX

In a quart-size reclosable bag, place:

1 cup alphabet pasta
1 tablespoon dried parsley
1 tablespoon onion powder

1 teaspoon garlic powder
1 cup powdered chicken soup base (or 4 chicken bouillon cubes)

Seal the bag, attach the tag on page 163, roll up and tie with a ribbon.

Little Red Hen—the children's classic

Any little child who loves to bake like mommy will love this classic nursery tale as well as the mix (ready for memory-making) for delicious homemade bread. First read about the little hen who does all the work herself, from planting the wheat to baking the bread, while her friends sit by lazily.

Then let the child check out the bags of dry bread mix set in their very own bread pan that's holding a checked kitchen towel and maybe their very own Little Red Hen ceramic figurine or plastic toy. Because the bread is mixed right in the bag, even preschoolers can handle this, leaving very little mess for Mom to clean up! Be sure to include the instructional tag on page 164.

WHOLE WHEAT BREAD IN A BAG

Dry mix bag #1—in a one-gallon reclosable bag, measure:

- 1   cup whole wheat flour
- 1   tablespoon bulk or 1 package of dry yeast
- 1   teaspoon salt

Seal the bag and gently shake until the ingredients are well mixed.

Dry mix bag #2—in a small reclosable bag include:

- 1   cup whole wheat flour

Mr. Popper's Penguins by Richard and Florence Atwater

This children's favorite tells about Mr. Popper, who loves to hear of Admiral Drake and his penguins at the South Pole. Imagine Mr. Popper's surprise when one day Admiral Drake sends him penguins of his very own! But how will he keep them in his small town? Read the book and see! Give this book in a Styrofoam ice bucket with the following items:

- a small stuffed penguin toy
- some store-bought Snowball cakes covered with coconut
- Klondike bars

- Ice Cube chocolate candies
- an atlas to search for the places mentioned in the book

Field Guide to North American Birds by The National Audubon Society

Young and old alike will enjoy this basket centered around bird-watching! Place the following items in a small backpack or fanny pack to take to the mountains, fields, or woods—anywhere birds of a feather gather together:

- binoculars
- bird seed
- a wooden birdhouse or kit to make one
- colored pencils
- a notebook for sketching birds, journaling, and noting the different birds spotted in your yard (how frequently, for what seasons, and with what habits)—a little research project

Nightlight: A Devotional for Couples by Dr. James & Shirley Dobson

This devotional for husbands and wives makes a great wedding or anniversary gift. Pair it with:

- a throw blanket
- a funky or beautiful nightlight, the style depending on the couple's personality
- two mugs
- hot chocolate (see p. 49 for mixes you can make) or Sleepytime tea
- bubble bath
- a candle

ADULT CHRISTIAN FICTION

There are so many wonderful novels available at your local Christian bookstore. If someone on your gift list loves to relax with a good book, give them one of the flavored coffee mixes from page 48 slipped into a cute mug and combined with a great book. Imagine: food for heart and soul!

Baskets & Bundles

A tisket, a tasket, what's in your basket? These ideas for baskets and bundles help you figure that out in a flash by centering around various themes or hobbies.

PACK & PLAY: A PLAN

Make a handy carrying bag to store your homemade play dough. First you'll need an oval-shaped vinyl place mat. On the back of the place mat, attach Velcro to the edges so that it will fold and stay shut. Then, for carrying handles, glue two pieces of cord to the rounded sides on the backside of the place mat.

When shut, the mat should look like a carrying bag. You can store play dough and cookie cutters inside this handy case that also serves as a working mat during play—protecting any tabletop, carpet, or floor where your child works.

RAINY DAYS

Play dough and pudding fingerpaints make a wonderful combination for encouraging creativity, especially a small child's. Put these items together for a great birthday gift. Include the following:

- chocolate, vanilla, or butterscotch pudding; include the boxes or make the puddings ahead of time and place in labeled, airtight containers
- colored construction paper or a box of wax paper for fingerpainting
- bags of homemade play dough in a variety of colors (see the recipe below)
- a laminated place mat to use as a play dough work area
- cookie cutters with the place mat's theme

KOOL-AID PLAY DOUGH

1	cup white flour
1	cup water
1	tablespoon vegetable oil
¼	cup salt
2	tablespoons cream of tartar
1	package Kool-Aid

Mix all ingredients in a saucepan and cook, stirring constantly, over medium heat 3 to 5 minutes. Soon a ball will form in the center. Knead on a floured surface. Store in a baggie.

WELCOME, NEIGHBOR!

When a new family moves into your neighborhood, be there to greet them with this! Gather the following items and place them in a basket:

- loaf of homemade quick bread or some muffins
- jar of jam
- change of address cards
- a map of the city or county
- a copy of the book *After the Boxes Are Unpacked* by Susan Miller—on surviving and thriving during relocation
- a small notebook full of local information, such as the phone number for your favorite local hairstylist, names and numbers of recommended doctors, the day and time of your block's trash pickup, directions to family attractions in the area, and the location and times of area church services
- a coupon they can redeem for a home-cooked meal with you (see p. 165)

THE BIG MOVE

If you have a friend who will be moving to another state, a perfect going-away gift would be a basket of food products that your city or state is known for. For instance, if your city is known for blueberries, fill a basket with things made from blueberries—blueberry jam, blueberry pie, blueberry gelatin or Kool-Aid, blueberry muffins, and even some fresh blueberries. Or maybe you would like to make a variety of foods using homegrown products from across the state. This will give your friend some great memories as he or she adapts to a new area.

JUST WHAT THE DOCTOR ORDERED

Anyone recovering from illness or surgery would be encouraged with the love packed in this basket:

- chicken soup in a jar (see the recipe below)
- a box of herbal tea, nestled in a cute mug
- a votive candle
- a box of soft tissues
- a bag of cough drops or lemon drops
- books or magazines
- an old movie or two on video

Be sure to attach the decorative gift tag, featuring Ephesians 3:16, on page 165.

OLD-FASHIONED CHICKEN SOUP

1	4-pound chicken, cut up
6	cups water
1	small onion, chopped
1	teaspoon salt
½	teaspoon pepper
½	teaspoon thyme
1	bay leaf
2	stalks celery, chopped
2	carrots, chopped
2	cups uncooked noodles

In a large Dutch oven, combine water, chicken, onion, salt, pepper, thyme, and bay leaf. Bring to a boil. Reduce heat and simmer for 2 hours. Take out bay leaf. Remove chicken from broth and cut off the bone. Skim off any fat from the top of the broth. Add celery, carrots, and noodles. Return to a boil and simmer for 8 minutes. Add chicken and simmer another 5 minutes. Let cool and place in quart canning jars. Keep refrigerated.

BEAUTIFUL FEET BASKET

Do you know someone who needs a little pick-me-up? Perhaps your pastor's wife or a Sunday school teacher? Give them a basket containing:

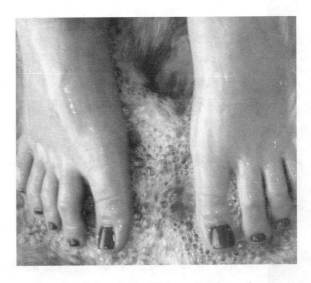

- apricot scrubbing lotion
- soothing foot cream
- a pumice stone or nail file
- a jar of nail polish
- pastel cotton socks or a pair of slippers
- a hand towel, rolled up and tied with a length of lace

Don't forget the tag inspired by Romans 10:15 on page 166: "How beautiful are the feet of those who bring good news!"

SPORTS NUTS

Use an old football helmet to send these treats to the sports fanatic in your life:

- submarine sandwiches
- Barbecued Nuts (use the recipe below)
- Southwestern Veggie Dip (see pp. 55 and 153)
- vegetables or nacho chips to dip
- a whistle
- sugar cookies cut in the shape of footballs (for a cookie cutter, bend the ends of an empty soup can slightly to form a football shape)

BARBECUED NUTS

4	cups unsalted, mixed nuts
½	cup smoke-flavored barbecue sauce
1	teaspoon onion salt
½	teaspoon onion powder

In a large bowl, combine all ingredients, mixing well. Spread nuts out on a greased cookie sheet. Bake 25 minutes at 300 degrees, stirring twice during baking. Remove from oven and allow to cool before transferring to container. Use the tag on page 166.

MOVIE NIGHT IN A BOX

For a fun evening give a Movie Night Box! Fill a large popcorn tub (ask for one at your local movie theater) with peanuts in the shell. Add a six-pack of old-fashioned bottled pop, some microwave popcorn packets, and everyone's favorite movie candies like you might find at an old-time movie house: Junior Mints, Jujyfruits, Jujubes, or Good & Plenty.

Include a home movie of your children and wrap the video in a light-colored piece of construction paper, decorated like an actual movie poster, complete with title, list of stars, the names of director and producer. Perhaps the title would be something like: *Three Busy Boys,* starring Steven, Austin, and Jonathan.

Use stamps or stickers to finish decorating your cover and make "movie tickets" from construction paper.

For faraway relatives, send just the movie and popcorn. What a great way to keep in touch!

ITALIAN PASTA DINNER BAG

For the pasta-lover in your life, provide a restaurant in a bag. Here are the items you will need:

- two or three kinds of pasta (spaghetti, bowtie, and linguine, for example)
- one jar of your favorite pasta sauce, prepackaged or homemade (see the recipe on p. 169)
- one can of Parmesan cheese
- one loaf of homemade or store-bought Italian bread
- large red-and-white-checked napkins
- a brown paper grocery bag
- brown lunch bags
- twine
- a sponge
- red and white paint

To decorate your bag, fold down the top twice and cut out two square cubes from a sponge. Paint onto the bag a red-and-white checkerboard pattern with the sponges. Put the various kinds of pasta in lunch bags, each secured with twine and labeled as to the kind of pasta contained.

Now make some pasta sauce bibs to catch those messy drips: Purchase some red-and-white-checked fabric (perhaps a 1-foot square for each person's bib). With pinking shears, cut out the bibs, and attach two pieces of twine to two corners. With craft-stitching paint, add on each bib the words "That's-a-nice-a pasta!" Add the remaining items.

BACKPACKER'S PACK

This is what to get for the active person who likes the outdoors and has everything:

- a map of local trails to hike
- trail mix (try mixing peanuts and chocolate chips or M&M's)
- a book on backpacking or hiking
- a compass (and the tag with John 14:6 on p. 166)
- bottled water (with the psalm-inspired tag on p. 167; "As the deer pants for streams of water, so my soul pants for you, O God.")

CARAMEL APPLE BASKET

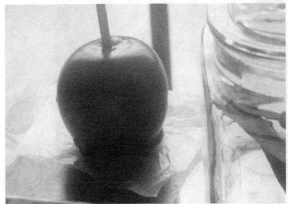

What could be a sweeter fall treat than caramel apples? For a quick, yet delicious gift that children will especially love, place apples, a bag of caramels, and a bag of craft sticks in a basket. For an extra-special finishing touch, include the gift tag on page 167, featuring Psalm 17:8.

PIZZA NIGHT BASKET

For a busy family, this basket is sure to bring some family fun time as they make their own pizza! Gather the following items and place them in a large basket:

- one 8-ounce can of pizza sauce
- one round chub of mozzarella cheese
- one 6-ounce can of mushrooms
- one stick of pepperoni
- one green pepper
- one medium-sized onion
- Handy Bread Mix (see recipe on p. 26) and include tag for Homemade Pizza (p. 135)
- red-and-white-checked paper plates and matching napkins
- a six-pack of soda pop
- one coupon good for the rental of a movie at a video store

THE ROAD TRIP

Any family that is leaving on vacation will welcome this gift, with all kinds of goodies sure to keep the kids busy for hours:

- books on tape (we love Adventures in Odyssey!)
- books (pick one up about your destination)
- snacks (keep special ones for crossing a state line or marking 100 miles)
- games for rest stops (Frisbees, balls and gloves, badminton)
- a roll of quarters for each child (each time there is any grumbling, fighting, or horseplay, one quarter is forfeited; the rest can be used to purchase souvenirs!)
- travel pillows
- activity books
- colored pencils
- disposable cameras, one for each child

LEMON BASKET

Do you have a loved one who's down because of a bad week at work? Or a coach whose sports team didn't win the tournament? This perfect pick-me-up will brighten their day! Put anything you can think of that has to do with lemons inside a basket and include the gift tag on page 169. Some of our basket favorites:

- old-fashioned lemon drops
- batch of Lemon Poppy Seed muffins or the Lemon Poppy Seed Muffin Mix on page 31
- Lemon Pepper Seasoning Mix from page 55
- a citrus juicer
- a few bags of lemon flavored tea
- any kind of lemon-scented soap or lotion
- fill in the basket with real lemons
- don't forget the punchline—a recipe for fresh lemonade

PRAYER BASKET

To encourage a special friend or new Christian to remain steadfast in practicing their faith, give them a prayer basket filled with inspiration:

- a journal to record their thoughts or to keep track of their prayer requests and God's answers
- a pretty pen and note cards for jotting a quick letter of encouragement to a fellow Christian
- a classic book like *Celebration of Discipline* by Richard Foster
- a mug or cup and saucer with tea bags or packets of flavored coffee tucked inside
- a pretty box of tissues and maybe a plush pair of socks for those cool early mornings
- a CD of soothing worship music
- a Bible with study helps in an easy-to-understand translation

FISHERS OF MEN BASKET

For that little fisherman (or fisher-woman!) in your life, find a rustic-looking basket or open tackle box (maybe even an old fishing creel) and fill it with:

- lures and bobbers
- gummy fish or worms, or fish-shaped crackers or pretzels
- a copy of the book *Pete, Feet and Fish to Eat* by Phil A. Smouse

Tuck in some pamphlets from your state's Department of Natural Resources on places to fish in your area. Don't forget the inspirational tag on page 167 featuring Matthew 4:19.

SWEET DREAMS

You can adapt this idea for an adult or a child by filling a basket (or maybe some beautiful or fun pillowcases!) with homey items to lull anyone into a sweet, sound sleep. For adult or child, don't forget the inspirational tag on page 153 featuring Proverbs 3:24.

For grown-ups include:

- chamomile tea
- a small pillow, either store bought or hand-stitched; if making your own, put some dried rosemary or lavender inside the pillow to encourage peaceful sleep

- an antique canning jar filled with homemade cookies with a pretty ribbon tied at the top
- hot cocoa mix
- sweet-smelling night cream or lotion
- a nightgown
- a copy of the book *Night Whispers: Bedtime Stories for Women* by Jennie Dimkoff

For children include:

- a half-pint of chocolate or strawberry milk
- Oreo cookies in a cellophane bag tied shut with a ribbon
- a teddy bear
- a new pair of pajamas
- a copy of one of these children's classics: *Goodnight Moon* by Margaret Wise Brown; *The Velveteen Rabbit* by Margery Williams; *How Do Dinosaurs Say Good Night* by Jane Yolen and Mark Teague; *Corduroy the Bear* by Don Freeman; or *Ten in the Bed* by Penny Dale

GOD'S BASKET OF LOVE

Find a medium-size basket and tie a pretty bow on the handle. Choose a person or family you want to give it to and fill the basket with something special just for them: food, flowers, a book. Now place inside or on the handle a copy of the tag on the right, along with a copy of the inspirational tag featuring John 13:34, found on page 156. Make arrangements for the basket to be secretly delivered so you remain anonymous. Stand back and watch God's love flow as the basket travels from home to home.

Inspired by John 13:34, this basket says, "You Are Loved," only without words. Take this gift and enjoy it as long as you wish: for a day, week, month, year, or longer—you decide. When you see another person sick, hurting, or just having a bad day, let them know how special and appreciated they are—take this basket and fill it with LOVE (and a plant, book, fruit, or other special thing) and have it delivered to them. Make sure to leave this note in the basket so that they, in turn, can pass it along too. Enjoy God's love today!

BRIDE'S BASKET

Help a bride celebrate her marriage with this special basket lined with tulle and tied with ribbons all in white—a sign of purity. If you have a daughter, don't wait till she's engaged to prepare this gift; start when she's young to collect just the right things over the years. Include an item for each part of this old familiar rhyme:

Something Old—a piece of family jewelry, embroidered handkerchief, or a garter

Something New—anything the bride will need to complete her attire

Something Borrowed—usually a family heirloom or treasured possession borrowed from the bride's family or from a close female friend

Something Blue—symbolizing faithfulness and loyalty, this "something" is commonly a blue or blue-trimmed garter

Silver Sixpence—since silver sixpence are less common today, brides usually use a penny in their left shoe

A mother could give this basket to her daughter at a bridal shower or share a quiet moment together before her wedding day. Don't forget to include the tag, featuring this beloved wedding day rhyme, on page 168.

A NEW MOM

Many times the gifts for a new baby are given exclusively to the little one. Surprise a mom with a basket filled with a few items just for her. As a mom adjusts to motherhood or an additional child, she'll feel blessed and encouraged that her role as a mother is seen as God's highest call in her life. Include in your basket any of the following:

- a "Mommy Book" or devotional
- *Mom's Devotional Bible*
- lullaby CD
- nursing gown
- slippers
- chamomile tea
- lotion
- Mom's favorite snack
- a card offering your help with the new baby or the other children while Mom enjoys a relaxing nap, bath, or quiet time
- a nutritious meal or two for the new mom to pull out of her freezer on an especially busy day

7

Bringing the
Outdoors In

· ·

A bouquet of dandelions. Fireflies in a jar. A bird's nest or an autumn leaf. Children seem to notice these things; they find simple beauty and pure joy in each element of the great outdoors. In our busyness, it's a beauty we adults too often miss—especially when it comes through the door in the shape of a creamy mud pie or a slimy toad, right?

Gifts inspired by nature can be powerful reminders of this truth: "Consider how the lilies grow. They do not labor or spin. Yet I tell you, not even Solomon in all his splendor was dressed like one of these" (Luke 12:27). With these fresh ideas there's no need to fret over what lovely gift to give someone. When you look for the beauty beyond your doorstep, you'll not only find it, you'll be eager to pass it along.

From Mulch
to Pretty Paper

With a few simple instructions you can make your own paper for beautiful, treasured, one-of-a-kind gifts.

Start with any paper scraps: old telephone books, used typing paper, newspapers; just about anything works. The ingredients you choose to add in can suit your whim: tiny leaves, squashed pinecone parts or thistles, hay or grass blades, string, ribbon or fabric bits, thread or yarn, and more. What a way to recycle!

Here's what you'll need:

- scraps of paper of any kind or papier-mâché mix
- a blender
- a basin at least 10 by 13 inches
- a fiberglass screen or regular window screen
  (cut screen into two 9-inch by 12-inch sheets)
- paper towels (plan to use lots; the cheaper brands work best for this because they mulch easier)
- assorted add-ins:
  wildflower seeds
  flower petals
  pine needles
  grass
  bits of thread or confetti

Make handcrafted paper using these 10 simple steps:

1. Gather the pieces of paper to be recycled. If it's a crisp, white paper you want to make, use papier-mâché mix from the craft store.

2. Tear the paper into small bits and put them in the blender so it's half full of the paper pieces. Now fill the blender to

the top with warm water. Put the lid on the blender and press START, slowly increasing speed as you go. Blend until the mixture looks smooth and well-mixed (maybe 1 minute). If you detect any paper flakes, keep blending.

3. Fill your basin about halfway with water. Add 3 blenders full of paper pulp and whatever add-ins you choose. Mix.

4. Place one sheet of screen into the basin and gently wiggle the screen from side to side until the pulp on top looks even.

5. Slowly lift the screen from the water and keep it over the basin until most of the water drains. A sheet of paper—albeit wet—should appear on top of the screen. If the new sheet looks too thick, remove some of the pulp from the basin, submerge the screen and go back to step 4. If the new sheet of paper looks too thin, add more pulp to basin and go back to step 4.

6. When the screen stops dripping, carefully lower it onto a pile of folded paper towels.

7. Place the other screen on top and cover with another layer of folded paper towels. Press down on the sheet of paper until the paper towels are saturated. Keep replacing paper towels until no more water remains on your new sheet of paper.

8. Put the screens, with your new sheet of paper inside, between two fresh paper towels. Stack up as many pieces of paper as you wish this way. Let dry at least two days.

9. Carefully peel the screen from your hand-pressed paper and see how your creation turned out! No two pieces will ever be exactly alike.

10. Use the paper for making stationery kits, greeting cards, or gift tags. Use the tag on page 168.

PLANT YOUR GOODWILL

Your kind greetings and words of affection can actually spread and grow with every card or letter on handcrafted paper.

Use lots of wildflower seeds in the next batch of handmade paper pulp that you mix. Then, once your paper is dried and ready for writing on, make a note on the back of each sheet: "This paper is made with love—and wildflower seeds. Plant it somewhere sunny, be sure to water the spot, and watch for flower power and know you're loved."

This is recycling at its best—and most beautiful.

T-Shirts—Naturally

You can make naturally beautiful T-shirts with just about anything from meadows, mountains, forests, streams, and even your own backyard. Children especially will love making this wearable art.

For a stenciled effect you'll need:

- a dark-colored T-shirt
- cardboard to fit the width of the shirt
- items from nature you want pictured on your T-shirt— flowers, leaves, pinecones, branches, rocks, or blades of grass
- a spray bottle filled with two parts water and one part bleach

For a pressed effect you'll need:

- a white T-shirt
- an old towel
- a bouquet of bright-colored flowers or green, fresh leaves or grasses
- a hammer
- a hot iron

To create a stenciled or outlined look: Lay the dark T-shirt on your driveway, garage floor, or other walkway. Place a piece of cardboard inside the shirt. Arrange large leaves or flowers on top of the shirt. Lightly spray the bleach mixture around the outside edges of the leaves or flowers. Let dry. Remove leaves and see your lovely, inverted image.

For the pressed or ingrained-color effect: Arrange a bouquet of colorful flowers on top of a white T-shirt. Carefully place a towel on top of the bouquet. Pound away with the hammer on the towel, pressing the natural pigments of the foliage into your shirt. Lift off the towel and discard the flowers. Press the T-shirt with a hot iron to heat-set this wearable bouquet!

Pressed Flowers

Remember that childhood pastime of pressing flowers in a telephone book, dictionary, or the Sears catalog? That same pressing method still works today and is an easy way to create lovely gifts.

Gather any flower petals or leaves that appeal to you. For the most colorful effect, look for a wide variety of shapes, sizes, and shades. Place the flowers between two paper towels or two sheets of wax paper and then between the pages of any large, heavy book. Leave the flowers to dry, pressed in the book, for about two weeks.

If the petals and stems do not feel or look dried after two weeks, leave them for one week more. Now look what you can make with this simple idea:

BOOKMARKS

Kids love making these simple, practical gifts. Just cut two pieces of clear self-adhesive paper a little larger than a bookmark. Peel off the paper backing. Place a few pressed flowers on one piece of the sticky paper. Lay the other one on top sticky side down. Trim the sides in any traditional or novelty shape, perhaps with decorative-edged scissors or pinking shears.

GROWING GRATITUDE

Remember that old line from the song "Count Your Blessings": "When my bank roll is getting small, I remember when I had none at all . . ."

It's true that there's always something to be grateful for.

Give someone who needs it most a reminder: On a piece of heavy paper, using two to three strands of embroidery floss, stitch the word "Blessings" in an uneven style with a simple running stitch. Don't trim your thread or worry about neatness. In fact, just tuck your needle into the paper when you're finished.

Now arrange a few pressed flowers in one corner and glue them in place.

Slip the paper into a simple frame and give this memento as a reminder that blessings are always works in progress and though we may be hard-pressed to see them, when one appears, like a wildflower, others will begin to bloom on the horizon too.

CANDLES

Turn plain candles into extraordinary giftable ones like you see in expensive department stores. You'll need:

- a smooth pillar candle, any size or color
- pressed flowers, leaves, fruit slices, or herbs
- a margarine container
- white glue
- a paintbrush
- enough paraffin wax to cover the pillar candle when it's dipped
- an old pan for melting the wax

On a piece of paper, arrange the pressed flowers into a bouquet or other design of your choosing—this is simply a helpful guide that you'll use. You might pencil around all the items you place so that when you remove them from the paper, you still have a visible pattern.

In a margarine container, mix four parts white glue with one part (or less) water. You want just enough water to thin the glue slightly. With the paint brush, spread a thin layer of glue on your candle where you want the pressed flowers to lay. Carefully place the flowers from your pattern onto the candle. Now, holding the wick, dip the entire candle into melted paraffin wax. Set the candle on wax paper or foil for the paraffin to dry and set. Include the accent tag on page 182, featuring Matthew 5:16: "Let your light shine before men, that they may see your good deeds and praise your Father in heaven."

FRAMES

Give an inexpensive frame a facelift with pressed petals and botanicals featured inside. All you need for this is any kind of frame, parchment paper or card stock, white glue, and your pressed materials. Beautiful ideas:

- a single autumn leaf
- a fringe of pine needles
- wide grass blades with a wildflower
- wispy herb leaves

Cut a piece of white parchment paper or card stock to the same size as the window of your frame and arrange pressed flowers in a bouquet or other design. When you are pleased with your arrangement, carefully glue (sparingly) the flowers onto the card stock. Let dry. Slip the featured flowers into the frame and you're done.

How Does Their Garden Grow?

You could give most gardeners a bag of dirt and they'd be happy. But these ideas are much more special than soil.

A gardening gift basket is easy to put together and is the perfect gift for those green of thumb. Just place some of the tools a gardener might need into a cute basket. These might include gardening gloves, hand cleanser and a scrub brush, hand lotion, a trowel, seed packages, wooden plant labels, even a bag of potting soil.

For a distinctive gift presentation, take a large terra-cotta pot and paint the outside with non-toxic, acrylic paint. In a contrasting color, stencil a design on the painted pot, and maybe a vine pattern around the rim. Now place your gift items right inside the pot. *Voila!* Great gifts and the perfect pot for a prized houseplant!

For either version don't forget the inspirational gift tag, featuring John 15:5, on pages 160 and 168: "I am the vine; you are the branches. If a man remains in me and I in him, he will bear much fruit; apart from me you can do nothing."

SPAGHETTI HERBS

New brides, old friends buying their first home, and college students venturing out on their own will all appreciate kitchen herb and spice starters. You can put together pre-packaged containers of these herbs along a creative theme—or simply reap them from your own herb garden and place them in tiny jars or baggies. Another idea—plant a variety of these herbs in one large terra-cotta pot for "Portable Spaghetti Spices":

- basil
- oregano
- parsley
- thyme
- garlic chives

You can also include a Roma tomato plant in a pot. However you give these herbs, be sure to include the instructional tag on page 169 for Homemade Spaghetti Sauce.

THE PIZZA GARDEN

This clever idea can get even the most anti-gardening child interested in planting and harvesting. In a clean pizza box, tape a combination of the following seeds side by side onto the bottom:

- tomatoes
- green peppers
- red peppers
- oregano
- parsley
- onions
- mild peppers
- thyme
- basil
- chives

Don't forget to attach the instructional tag on page 169. Also, be sure to give this gift early enough in the spring for transplanting time, especially if your recipient lives in a cool climate, where it's important to start plants early in the summer or even indoors.

THE PETER RABBIT GARDEN

Give a basket of seeds centered around the children's classic *Peter Rabbit* by Beatrix Potter. Remind your recipient what Peter finds when he wanders off into Mr. MacGregor's garden:

- onions
- carrots
- lettuce
- cabbage
- radishes
- parsley

Include packets of these seeds, along with a child's trowel, gardening gloves, and either a copy of the book or the video of the same name (we recommend the one produced by Goodtimes Home Videos). Also include chamomile tea. (Peter's mom gave him a cup of it when he returned home with a stomachache from eating too many vegetables.) For an adult, include the Carrot Cake Mix from page 34, along with its instructional tag on page 143.

SEEDS, SEEDS, SEEDS

Packets of seeds will grow on you as a versatile gift. How can you use them for gifts? Just let us count the ways:

- For a quick pick-me-up, tuck a package of seeds into a card. How about forget-me-nots for the friend who's moving away or baby's breath for the new mom?
- Make a mini wall hanging to carry your seed gifts. Take an old pair of blue jeans (use a pair with the holes in the knees!) and cut around the back pocket, leaving the back of the jeans and the pocket together. Poke a hole in each corner and make a hanger out of jute twine; simply thread each end through a hole and tie a knot. Tuck your seed packet right inside the pocket. Cute!

Give a package of lettuce seeds or a bag of ready salad greens with your very own Honey Mustard Dressing (see p. 170) and the instructional tag on page 170 that features Matthew 17:20: "I tell you the truth, if you have faith as small as a mustard seed, you can say to this mountain, 'Move from here to there' and it will move. Nothing will be impossible for you."

BLOOMS IN A BUCKET

For winter color, force the blooms of an amaryllis with this easy kit. Buy a small galvanized bucket at the discount store (or look for one at garage sales). Pour a layer of pebbles in the bottom. Place a couple of amaryllis bulbs on top and tie onto the bucket handle a small garden tool such as a hand trowel. Be sure to include the reminder (see the instructional note on p. 170) to "just add water."

WINDOW GARDEN

You don't need a plot of land or even a flower bed to be a gardener. Give everything for a little windowsill garden to a city-bound friend or someone who's shut-in.

Fill a gardening apron with some of these seeds for easy-to-grow herbs:

- basil
- chives
- cilantro
- garlic chives
- tarragon
- oregano
- rosemary
- sage
- spearmint (beware—this will spread easily)
- thyme
- parsley

Include a bag of potting soil, a planter, a bag of small rocks for drainage at the bottom of the container, and the instructional tag on page 171.

HUMMINGBIRD BASKET

Funny, isn't it, that you have to stay still in order to sit and watch the wing-beating frenzy of a hummingbird? But what fun! Children and adults alike love to watch these feathered friends; why not give your loved one a gift that keeps hummingbirds at hand? Fill a basket with a hummingbird feeder and seeds for plants that will attract the tiny birds:

- hollyhocks
- red impatiens
- snapdragon
- red columbine
- Indian paintbrush
- daylilies
- trumpet vine
- bleeding heart

BUTTERFLY GARDEN BASKET

Create a Butterfly Garden Basket similar to the Hummingbird Basket. Add a butterfly house and seed packets for plants that will attract butterflies:

- purple coneflower
- peonies
- lilacs
- yarrow
- nasturtiums
- asters
- French marigolds
- a butterfly bush (of course!)

For extra sweetness, include the CD or the children's book *Butterfly Kisses*— both by Bob Carlisle.

TRACKER'S BACKPACK

For the animal lover or critter sitter who loves a walk in the woods, give a fun-filled backpack for a day on the trail exploring God's creation:

- a book on animal tracks
- children's binoculars
- a notebook for drawing and journaling
- a set of colored pencils
- plaster of paris for making casts of animal tracks
- a magnifying glass

Buy a half gallon of Moose Tracks or Bear Claw ice cream to enjoy after the nature hike!

Fresh and Fruity Ideas

Use these garden-fresh ideas to make small hostess gifts, party favors, or door prizes. They're sure to please!

GREAT GLOWING GARDEN DELIGHTS!

Make cute apple candleholders that can begin on the table as an autumn accent and end up feeding the birds. Use an apple corer to cut a hole 1^1/$_2$ inches deep into various shapes and colors of apples. Work a taper candle into each hole. Display the candleholders on a runner made of a fall plaid fabric.

You can also use this idea with miniature pumpkins and gourds, substituting mini-sprays of wildflowers or garden greens for candles. What lovely, biodegradable vases you've created, my dear!

ARTICHOKE ART

Place a fresh artichoke in a small terra-cotta pot, stemside down. Cut a hole in the center large enough to hold a small pillar candle. Who would have known an artichoke could lighten your mood so?

A BOTANICAL BEAUTY

Use double-sided tape to secure bay leaves side by side around the exterior of several small votive candle cups. Add votive candles and tie the cups with shimmery gold or silver ribbon.

A CITRUS CENTERPIECE

For a spring bridal shower or garden party, slice various citrus fruits in half: oranges, grapefruits, and limes in particular. Lay them, cut side up, on a pretty crystal platter, with a hole carved in the pulp large enough to fit a votive candle. This beautiful centerpiece makes a lovely door prize or gift for days of fragrant enjoyment!

8

HEART-FILLED HOLIDAYS

· ·

Who doesn't scramble for gifts during the holidays? Okay, maybe Scrooge. Then again, by the end of his story even he was hustling to get the goose for a Christmas dinner gift.

This chapter might have helped him—and it certainly can keep you from having to trek to the mall. Whether you need a fresh, new idea for the old standby on your list or something special for a new acquaintance, the perfect gift may be closer to your fingertips than you think. So, go ahead and stir up some hot cocoa, put on your scratchy Bing Crosby Christmas album, and light a candle. You really can put together holiday gifts in the comfort of your own home.

Heartwarming Harvest

You see the signs on the cusp of every holiday season: The stores start rearranging departments, decorating in holiday themes, and displaying extra-special eats. For a little time, a lot less money, and with more care, you can make several of these specialty items. This section features recipes with a twist—your personal touch—for some popular harvest treats.

SCARECROW KIT

Get into the harvesttime spirit and give a basket filled with everything needed to make a scarecrow. You'll be helping a family have fun together and make memories. You may want to hit area garage sales or secondhand stores to purchase the needed materials:

- a flannel shirt
- a pair of jeans or overalls
- canvas garden gloves
- a straw hat
- old boots
- a pillowcase with a scarecrow face painted on it
- old rags or an actual bale of hay

Don't forget to attach the accent tag on page 171.

ALL-DAY APPLE BUTTER

5½	pounds apples, peeled and finely chopped
2½ to 4	cups sugar, adjusted to taste
3	teaspoons ground cinnamon
¼	teaspoon ground cloves
¼	teaspoon salt

Place apples in a large (6-quart) slow cooker. Combine spices and sugar and pour over apples. Mix well, cover, and cook on high for 1 hour. Reduce heat to low and cook covered for 9 to 11 hours or until thickened and dark brown. Stir occasionally to prevent sticking. Uncover and cook on low 1 hour longer. Stir with a wire whisk until smooth. Spoon into freezer containers, leaving 1 inch head space. Cover and refrigerate or freeze. Makes 4 pints. Don't forget the decorative tag on page 173.

Note: Tart cooking apples, such as Granny Smith, Macintosh, or Cortland, work best. Do not use eating apples such as Red Delicious or Gala.

SPICED CIDER MIX

This spicy mixture will warm any heart! Give it with either of the donut ideas that follow for a delicious treat.

- 10 cinnamon sticks, broken up
- 1 teaspoon whole cloves
- 2 tablespoons whole allspice

Mix all ingredients in a small bowl. Cut three 7-inch squares of cheesecloth and layer them. Place the spice mixture on the top. Gather the four corners and tie with string. Attach the instructional tag on page 172.

REFRIGERATOR BISCUIT DONUTS

This is so easy! Give this with Spiced Cider Mix for a taste of fall's finest flavors.

- 2 tubes of jumbo refrigerator biscuits
- 1 small paper lunch sack with cinnamon sugar
- 1 small paper lunch sack with powdered sugar

Place biscuits and lunch sacks with sugar in a small basket. Include the instructional tag on page 172.

APPLE CIDER DONUTS

Sample these delicious donuts, then mix up a batch to give away. This is an extra-special treat when given with a gallon of cider.

- 3¼ cups all-purpose flour
- ⅔ cup sugar
- 2 teaspoons baking powder
- 1½ teaspoons cinnamon
- 1 teaspoon ground nutmeg
- 1 teaspoon salt

Mix all ingredients together. Place in a gallon reclosable bag. Include the decorative, instructional recipe tag on page 172.

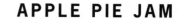

APPLE PIE JAM

Are you wondering what you can do to let your child's Sunday school teacher know what a blessing he or she is? This tasty jam loaded with chunks of apples and raisins will do the trick. Place this in three pint jars, then place a circle of pretty fabric on top of the lid and secure with a twine bow.

If you have a food dehydrator, dry some apple slices to glue to the top of the bow (cut the apple across the middle and you'll see a lovely star).

Don't forget to attach the accent tag on page 173.

3½	cups Granny Smith apples, peeled and chopped
½	cup raisins
¾	cup water
2	tablespoons lemon juice
2	teaspoons cinnamon
1	box fruit pectin
½	teaspoon butter
4	cups sugar
1	cup brown sugar

Place the fruit, water, and lemon juice in a saucepan. Add all remaining ingredients, except the sugars, and bring to a boil, stirring constantly. Now quickly stir in sugars. Bring to a rolling boil and continue boiling exactly 1 minute, stirring constantly. Remove the pan from heat. Ladle quickly into hot jars. Cover with hot lids and rings. Process the jars in a hot water bath for 10 minutes. Remove from the canner and let cool 24 hours.

Leave Them Thankful

If ever a holiday helped convey the Christian spirit of generosity, Thanksgiving's the one. You can give a friend any of the following gifts along with your thoughts on things you're thankful for—including great gift ideas like these.

BREAD CORNUCOPIA

This is not only a good treat to eat but pretty to look at as well. You could make it as a centerpiece for a holiday potluck and leave it with the host.

    2   loaves frozen wheat bread dough
    1   egg mixed with 1 tablespoon water
        a cone-shaped metal food sieve, covered in foil and sprayed with nonstick spray

Thaw and roll out both loaves of dough into rectangles about 10 by 16 inches. Leave one whole and cut the other one into strips the short way. Wrap the rectangular one around the foil-covered cone.

Using the egg wash as glue, paste the strips in a woven lattice fashion over the first loaf. You may cut one of the strips into three skinny strips and then braid them to glue along the opening of the cornucopia.

Wash the whole finished piece with egg and bake about 20 minutes at 350 degrees until just browned. Cool and remove cone and foil. Use as a centerpiece to serve Oatmeal Dinner Rolls.

OATMEAL DINNER ROLLS

2	cups water
1	cup quick oats
3	tablespoons butter
1	tablespoon yeast (one package)
⅓	cup warm water
⅓	cup brown sugar
1	tablespoon sugar
1	teaspoon salt
4¾ to 5¼	cups bread flour

Boil the 2 cups water and add oats and butter, stirring for one minute. Cool to lukewarm. Mix ⅓ cup warm water with yeast and sugars. Mix with oat mixture in a large bowl. Add salt and enough flour to make stiff dough. Knead the dough on a floured board for about 10 minutes (or in a mixer with a dough hook). Place in an oiled bowl and cover with a cloth. Let rise 1½ hours or until doubled.

Punch down the dough and shape it into 18 balls. Place the rolls in a greased 9- by 13-inch pan. Cover the rolls and let the dough rise again until sides touch one another, about 45 minutes.

Bake at 350 degrees for 20 minutes or until lightly golden. Serve in the Bread Cornucopia for a stunning presentation.

SEASONED RICE MIX

This mix-from-a-jar makes a great accompaniment to any poultry dish, especially one made with—you guessed it—leftover turkey. For a really unique jar topper, tie a dried corn husk around the rim. Otherwise just slip a ribbon or raffia bow around the rim of the jar.

3	cups brown or white long grain rice	¼	cup parsley flakes
2	tablespoons chicken bouillon granules	2	teaspoons onion powder
		½	teaspoon garlic powder
		¼	teaspoon thyme

Combine all ingredients in a quart jar with a tight-fitting lid, and don't forget the instructional tag on page 173.

PUMPKIN PECAN BUTTER

This is so tasty—like slices of your two favorite pies combined. Enjoy this butter in a variety of ways: on toast, muffins, and even pancakes. This recipe makes 5 half-pints (or 5 cups total) to give to friends or family. Place a pumpkin print fabric circle on top of the jar and secure with raffia. Tie a short cinnamon stick into the ribbon for the cherry-on-top touch. Don't forget the accent tag on page 174.

3½	cups canned pumpkin		substitute for pumpkin pie spice:
1	cup chopped pecans	1½	teaspoons cinnamon
1	tablespoon pumpkin pie spice	½	teaspoon nutmeg
4½	cups sugar	½	teaspoon ground cloves
1	box fruit pectin	½	teaspoon ginger
1	teaspoon butter		

Place all ingredients except sugar in a saucepan. Bring to a boil on high heat, stirring constantly. Quickly stir in all sugar. Return to a boil and boil exactly one minute, stirring constantly. Remove from heat. Skim off any foam with a metal spoon. Quickly ladle into hot jars and place hot lids and rings on, screwing firmly. Process jars for 10 minutes in a hot water bath. Remove from the canner and let cool for 24 hours.

PUMPKIN DIP

Another pumpkin-flavored favorite! This is a wonderful treat to take to a fall harvest party. The recipe makes 7 cups—enough for a couple of parties, or to share with friends. Bring a bag of purchased gingersnaps to go along with the dip. A cute addition to your jar would be an antique teaspoon tied into a bow of red or orange ribbon. Don't forget the accent tag on page 174.

    4   cups powdered sugar
   16   ounces cream cheese, softened
    1   30-ounce can pumpkin
    2   teaspoons cinnamon
    1   teaspoon ginger

In a large bowl, combine sugar and cream cheese, beating well. Add remaining ingredients. Store in the refrigerator. To serve, place in a small pumpkin that has been hollowed out. Enjoy!

HOMESTYLE STUFFING MIX

Make this for Thanksgiving dinner, whether it's at your place or someone else's. Just place ingredients in a quart jar and top with a circle of fall plaid fabric. Secure the fabric circle with jute twine. Include the recipe tag on page 174.

   3½   cups dried, cubed bread
    3   tablespoons dried celery flakes
    2   tablespoons dried parsley
    1   tablespoon dried minced onion
    2   teaspoons instant chicken
        bouillon granules
    ½   teaspoon poultry seasoning
    ½   teaspoon sage

Place the cubed bread in a quart jar. Combine remaining ingredients and place in a snack-size reclosable bag. Fold the bag and place it on top of the bread in the jar. Close the lid and decorate.

THE ART OF THANKSGIVING

Looking for something to keep the kids busy while you prepare the Thanksgiving feast?

Roll out some brown or white craft or butcher paper, give the children plenty of crayons or washable markers, and set them to work creating a Thanksgiving mural.

Suggest drawings of things each child is thankful for or ask each child to draw scenes of his or her interpretation of the first Thanksgiving feast with the Pilgrims and Indians. Save the mural and give it to next year's Thanksgiving host as a topper for the kids' table.

TURKEY NOODLE SOUP

Surprise whoever hosts Thanksgiving dinner this year with the perfect "thank you"—Turkey Noodle Soup Mix! Your host will be grateful for this convenient way to use leftover turkey! Tie a wooden spoon into a raffia bow and include the instructional tag on page 175.

Layer the following in a quart jar:

- ¼ cup powdered chicken soup base (if you cannot find powdered soup base mix, substitute 4 chicken bouillon cubes and place them as the last layer in the jar, still wrapped)
- 2 envelopes onion-mushroom soup mix
- ⅓ cup split peas
- 3 cups or more old-fashioned hearty egg noodles or dumplings

THANKSGIVING TABLE RUNNER

For a special, memory-making heirloom, simply take a piece of muslin fabric and cut a piece 12 inches wide by 36 inches long. Sew a ½-inch hem around all edges. At your next family gathering, place this table runner in the middle of the table with a selection of permanent markers or fabric markers. Have each person present write something on the runner that they are thankful for. Each year, get this table runner out to display. Enjoy the old memories and add some new ones!

Our Favorite Things

Though many of the following gifts would be welcome any time of year, they're especially appropriate in December. The added bonus: You'll find ingredients and elements for many of these special treats at great prices around Christmastime!

MARINATED ITALIAN CHEESE

This makes a beautiful hostess gift. Just tie a bow around the rim of the jar with red ribbon (raffia looks great) and be sure to include the accent tag on page 176.

- 1 16-ounce block mozzarella cheese, cut into 1-inch cubes
- 2 cups olive oil
- 1 red and 1 green pepper, cut into thin strips
- ¼ cup vinegar
- 1 tablespoon oregano leaf flakes
- 1 tablespoon basil leaf flakes
- 1 teaspoon thyme leaf flakes
- 3 cloves garlic, halved

Prick each cheese cube with a fork. Place the cubes, dividing evenly, into 3 or 4 decorative jars with tight-fitting lids.

In a saucepan, heat the rest of the ingredients until just warm. Cool completely and pour over cheese. Place lids on and store in the fridge one week before giving. This will keep for 6 weeks. Bring to room temperature before serving. Note: Do not use ground spices in this recipe.

CANDY CANE CRUNCH

- 24 ounces vanilla or almond bark
- 2 cups crushed candy canes

Crush the candy canes in a food processor or place the candy canes in a reclosable bag and crush with a rolling pin. Melt the bark in the microwave on high for 2 minutes, stirring often (or in a pan on a stovetop, on low heat). Stir in the crushed candy canes and pour the mixture into a jelly roll pan. Cool the candy. Break it into pieces and place in a cellophane bag; tie shut with a white ribbon.

CRANBERRY WALNUT RELISH

Place this pretty relish in 3 pint jars. Using a needle and sturdy thread, string enough cranberries to fit around the rim of the jar. Tie the string where the cranberries meet; using the same thread or a separate ribbon, tie on a copy of the decorative tag on page 176.

    5   cups cranberries
    2   cups water
    ½   cup chopped walnuts
    4½   cups sugar
    2   teaspoons cinnamon
    1   teaspoon nutmeg
    1   teaspoon allspice
    1   box fruit pectin
    ½   teaspoon butter

In a large kettle, bring the berries and water to a boil. Reduce heat and simmer for 10 minutes. Stir in walnuts, spices, pectin, and butter. Bring to a boil on high heat, stirring constantly. Quickly stir in all the sugar. Return to a boil for exactly 1 minute.

Remove from heat and skim off any foam. Ladle quickly into hot jars and secure the hot lids and rings, screwing them on firmly. Process the jars in a hot water bath for 10 minutes. Remove jars from the canner and let cool on a counter for 24 hours. Makes 6 cups.

MUG MAT

A natural aromatic air freshener and cuter than an ordinary coaster, a mug mat makes the perfect complement to any of the flavored coffee or hot chocolate mixes on pages 48–49.

    1   7- by 13-inch rectangle of any fabric (heavier-weight fabrics like denim or corduroy
         work best)
    2   large cinnamon sticks
    2   tablespoons whole cloves

With right sides together, fold the rectangle in half so that you have a 7- by 6½-inch piece. Leaving a 2-inch opening, sew a half-inch seam around the remaining edges. Turn right side out. In a small bowl, break up the cinnamon sticks and add the cloves. Carefully pour these spices into the fabric pouch's 2-inch opening. Stitch the opening closed. Place a cup of hot tea on the mat and smell the fragrances!

CANDY CANE CAPPUCCINO

- 1 cup powdered non-dairy creamer
- 1⅓ cups sugar
- 1 cup instant coffee
- 1 cup hot cocoa mix
- 8 regular-size candy canes

Blend all ingredients in a blender or food processor until a smooth powder results. Place the mix in a container or bag decorated with a red bow and a small candy cane. Don't forget the accent tag on page 177.

OATMEAL CHRISTMAS PANCAKES

Wake up your family Christmas morning with the mouthwatering aroma of these tasty pancakes—your special gift of time and effort to them.

Or give this hearty breakfast gift to friends or neighbors by placing ingredients in jars. Fold a new green-and-red dishcloth into fourths and place on top of the jar; secure it with a twine bow. For a cute accent, tuck a sprig of evergreen or a pancake turner or wooden spoon into the bow. You could also include some maple syrup or a jar of the Apple Pie Jam from page 110. Don't forget the instructional tag on page 176.

- 4 cups quick cooking oats (run them through a blender to make a flour-like powder)
- 2 cups flour
- 2 cups whole wheat flour
- 1 cup brown sugar
- 1 cup nonfat dry milk powder
- 3 tablespoons baking powder
- 2 tablespoons cinnamon
- 5 teaspoons salt
- ½ teaspoon cream of tartar

Combine all ingredients in a large bowl. This recipe makes enough mix to fill 5 pint jars or 2 quart jars plus 1 pint jar.

KEEPING CHRISTMAS ON HAND

Christmas is the perfect time to share the love of Christ with those He has put into our lives. Part of having a well-stocked gift-giving pantry is having a supply of small gift items on hand for those visitors who may drop in—a family on its way through town, the mail carrier, the newspaper carrier. A small remembrance can help these people know how much they mean both to you and to the God who created them. So, take any of the recipes in this book—layered mixes and canned jams work especially well—and make a few extra. Then when you hear someone knock on the door, you'll be prepared with something special just for them!

GINGERBREAD MAN KIT

This is such a cute gift to delight children and kids at heart. Just tuck the following items into a basket:

- Gingerbread Man Cookie Mix (recipe below)
- a gingerbread man cookie cutter
- assorted frostings in airtight containers
- assorted items to decorate cookies, such as small candies, raisins, cloves for eyes, etc.

GINGERBREAD MAN COOKIES

5	cups all-purpose flour
1½	teaspoons baking soda
½	teaspoon salt
1	tablespoon ground ginger
1	teaspoon ground cinnamon
1	teaspoon ground cloves

Mix all ingredients in a large bowl. Place in a gallon-size reclosable bag. Present in a basket with the items listed above. An instructional gift tag is provided on page 178.

SHORTBREAD

This is not only tasty, it's a quick gift to fix when you need something special but simple.

3	sticks real butter
¾	cup sugar
3	cups flour

Mix all ingredients and place the dough in a well-greased 9-inch square pan. Score the top for cutting guidelines and prick with a fork. Bake at 375 degrees for 15 to 20 minutes. Cool slightly and cut while still warm. Cool completely and store in a covered container.

GRANDMA'S SNOWBALLS

Use a quart jar for these cookies. For the jar topper, take a child's red sock and turn it inside out. Cut off the toe end and tie a bit of string around the opening. Pull tight and knot. Turn the sock right side out. Now fold up the cuff of the sock to form a little red, knit hat. Place the hat on the top of the jar lid. For extra appeal glue a jingle bell or pom-pom to the end of the hat. Wasn't that easy? And so cute!

$\frac{7}{8}$ cup (not quite a full cup) butter, softened
3 tablespoons powdered sugar
$1\frac{7}{8}$ cups flour
1 cup ground pecans (very finely chopped)
1 teaspoon vanilla

Mix all ingredients well and roll into balls. Bake on an ungreased cookie sheet at 300 degrees for 40 minutes. Cool slightly and place in a small paper bag with powdered sugar; close the bag and shake. Store in a covered container at room temperature.

HANDMADE STOCKINGS

Are you looking for an adorable gift bag? Or a truly one-of-a-kind stocking for each of your children? Create your own that will be all the more beloved because you sewed them yourself!

Trace a stocking shape on a large piece of paper. Lay this pattern on top of a double layer of fabric with right sides out (try felt, quilted material, canvas, or a Christmas print). Pin your pattern onto your fabric. Cut a half-inch outside of your pattern line with pinking shears. Machine stitch a half-inch seam around the sides and bottom, leaving the top open. Embellish your creation with craft paint, embroidery, buttons, or sprigs of evergreen.

CREATE YOUR OWN WRAPPING PAPER

Just run out of wrapping paper? No need to trek to the store. You can make beautiful wraps that are unique, one-of-a-kind, and a gift in their own right.

- **Let it snow:** Lay paper doilies on plain red wrapping paper. Using white spray paint, give a quick spray over the doilies. Use a very light touch. When dry, remove the doilies and, look—beautiful snowflakes!
- **Stamp-o-rama:** You can find cute stamps (angels, trees, stars, presents, holly berries and twinkly light shapes) and rolls of craft or butcher paper that are inexpensive. You might even use plain, brown packaging paper (found in the mailing aisle of a drugstore). Spread the paper on a table and, using a stamp pad or craft paint, stamp away. Try stamping angels or stars onto solid blue paper using silver, metallic craft paint.
- **Marble mania:** Now it's time to get your little ones in on the act. Place large pieces of plain rolled paper on a cookie sheet. Let the kids dip marbles into craft paint. Place the marbles on the paper and tilt the cookie sheet so the marbles roll around, making patterns. Boys especially love to roll the wheels of small cars through the paint and then on the paper. Experiment, have fun, create beautiful paper, and make a memory all at the same time.

DECORATIVE CANDLES

Decorative candles like the ones you see in department stores don't have to cost an arm and a leg. By making your own, you can save money and personalize each present. You'll need:

- a store-bought white pillar candle
- paraffin wax
- a large can with smooth sides, slightly larger in diameter than the candle
- a pan to melt the wax (you won't want to use this for cooking again!)
- add-ins:
    peppermints or small candy canes
    coffee beans
    broken cinnamon sticks
    buttons
    confetti

Place the candle in the center of the can. Around the candle pour in your add-ins, filling about halfway. Over low heat, melt the wax. Carefully pour melted wax over your add-ins. Let cool and harden before attempting to remove from can.

THE CENTERPIECE

When entertaining, fill a medium-size glass bowl with fresh cranberries. Add water to about three inches in depth. Arrange in the pool of berries these organics: fresh ivory and burgundy roses along with holiday greens like holly, ivy, and pine branches. Place additional small fruits like crabapples or fresh cherries and large nuts in the shell (walnuts look nice) within the greenery. Place several ivory candles of varying heights around the outside of the bowl. Be sure to send this pretty bowl home with one of your guests.

ICE LUMINARIES

Fire and ice—now that can be a bigger surprise than any present! Create ice luminaries by centering a 2-inch diameter candle in a clean half-gallon, cardboard (not plastic) milk carton. Stuff holly around the edges, using it to center and hold the candle. Fill the carton with water, making sure the wick is well above the edge of the carton, and freeze solid.

To remove the paper, dip the carton in warm water for a few seconds and peel it away. Keep the luminary frozen until ready to use. Then place it in a shallow glass bowl or tray and cluster more holly around the base.

Light the candle and watch your centerpiece melt down throughout the evening. You can also make an ice luminary with slices of fresh citrus fruit for a different look!

GIVE A PIECE OF YOUR HEART

For a unique way to give this fudge to a friend, place a metal cookie cutter on a piece of wax paper. Use a heart-shaped one for Valentine's Day or a bell, star, or gingerbread man for Christmas.

Pour the fudge into the cookie cutter, filling it about three-fourths of the way to the top. While still warm, sprinkle on colored candy bits, sparkly red sugar, or decorative-shaped sprinkles.

Once cooled, remove the wax paper. Place the fudge-filled cookie cutter in a small cellophane bag and tie it shut with curling ribbon or a length of torn calico material.

Days of Twine & Roses

For Valentine's Day, your anniversary, or your beloved's birthday, the next best thing to roses is chocolate. When tied up with a little ribbon or twine, one of these ideas will make a sweet gift.

FUDGE FOR NO-BRAINERS

This recipe is so easy, and it's a winner with any chocolate lover.

3   cups good quality semi-sweet chocolate chips
1   can sweetened condensed milk
1   teaspoon vanilla

In a saucepan, melt the chocolate chips and milk on low. Stir in vanilla. Pour into a foil-lined pan. For a loaf of fudge, use a 9-inch loaf pan. If you prefer fudge squares, pour into an 8-inch square pan. Double this recipe for a 9- by 13-inch pan.

You can also experiment with mint, orange, or cherry extracts. Or use milk chocolate or peanut butter chips.

For an extra special treat, make two recipes of fudge, one using white chocolate chips and one using dark chocolate chips. Then either layer them in a 9- by 13-inch pan or pour both kinds in and swirl them together.

CHOCOLATE RASPBERRY SPREAD

- 5 cups raspberries, crushed
- 7 cups sugar
- 1 box fruit pectin
- 5 squares unsweetened chocolate
- ½ teaspoon butter

Measure berries into a large saucepan. Stir pectin into fruit. Add chocolate and butter. Bring to a boil, stirring constantly. Quickly stir in all sugar. Return to a full rolling boil for exactly one minute, stirring constantly. Remove from heat and skim off any foam.

Quickly ladle the mixture into clean, hot jars. (Keep the jars standing in hot water in the sink.)

Cover the jars with lids and screw on the rings firmly but do not overtighten. Process the sealed jars in a hot water bath for 10 minutes. Remove them from the canner and let cool at room temperature for 24 hours.

This recipe makes 9 cups.

Don't forget to top the jars with ribbon or a fabric topper and the accent tag on page 180.

GIFTS THAT CAN'T BE WRAPPED

Make a list of people you know who need encouragement: maybe a neighbor struggling financially or a widow facing her first holiday season alone. Then set aside a night for your family to work on gifts for these folks.

Form an assembly line to fill jars. For instance, if you're mixing up some recipes in a jar, one person fills the jar with the first ingredient of a layered mix, the next person puts in the second, and the person at the end of the line adds the ribbon. Have everyone sign a card or tag.

This idea also works wonderfully as Sunday school classes get together to make gifts for elderly shut-ins. Or invite a friend over—have her bring her kids and you can tackle both your gift lists together. Fun and productive—and you'll be giving to those you work alongside the gift of a lesson in generosity and service.

PEANUT BUTTER CUPS

Trust us, ladies, these are the way to your man's heart!

24	ounces milk chocolate chips (not semi-sweet)
1	cup natural creamy peanut butter
½	stick (¼ cup) butter, softened
2	cups powdered sugar
2	dozen foil muffin liners (small ones work best)

Mix peanut butter and butter, in a small bowl. Add powdered sugar until mixture is the consistency of the inside of a store-bought peanut butter cup.

In a medium saucepan on low, slowly melt the chocolate chips. Place foil muffin liners in muffin tins. Using a pastry brush, completely brush the insides of muffin liners with a medium layer of the melted chocolate. Place the muffin tins in the freezer for a few minutes to harden the muffin liners.

Once semi-frozen, remove and fill not quite to the top with peanut butter filling. Then swirl more chocolate on top, being sure to touch the sides. Place the pan of peanut butter cups in the freezer again to harden.

Once hardened and set, store in a covered container in the refrigerator until ready to wrap and give.

CHOCOLATE TRUFFLES

1	12-ounce bag milk chocolate chips
½	cup heavy whipping cream
1	tablespoon butter
½	teaspoon vanilla, orange, mint, or almond extract assorted garnishes: chopped nuts, coconut, sprinkles, etc.

Over low heat, melt butter and cream (be careful not to scorch!). Stir in chips and extract until smooth. Cool slightly. Form into 1-inch balls and roll in garnishes. Keep in covered container in the refrigerator.

For you —
with love

9

Basics for Beginners

· ·

*E*xperience can make you an expert gift-maker—one homespun idea that you tackle at a time. These tips can help along the way.

Canning

For those of you unfamiliar with the dos and don'ts of canning, here's your cheat sheet:

BEFORE YOU BEGIN

Use only jars designed for canning. Never reuse mayonnaise, spaghetti sauce, or peanut butter jars.

Purchase lids and rings in the canning section of your grocery store. You may reuse the rings, but the lids are designed for one-time use only.

As you prepare a recipe for canning, you must keep the rings, lids, and jars hot. This can be done a couple of ways: Put the rings and lids in a small saucepan with enough water to cover and simmer on low. The jars can be kept standing in very hot tap water in the sink or in your dishwasher on the rinse and hold cycle.

AS YOU GO

Do not alter a recipe or reduce the amount of sugar and do not use sugar substitutes. Each ingredient is carefully measured for the balance of best preserving canned foods.

Once you've made a recipe, carefully ladle the mixture into hot jars. A canning funnel works well here. Be sure to wipe the rim clean with a lint-free washcloth dipped in hot water.

Carefully place a lid on the jar. Screw on the canning ring firmly but do not overtighten! You can find magnetic wands (in the canning section of grocery stores) that help remove the lids and rings from the hot water.

Make sure the large pot or "canner" you use is half full of hot water when you start to load it. Now place seven jars on the canning rack of your water bath canner. The rack is designed to either go all the way into the canner or to hook on the sides, suspending the rack about halfway up the canner. This is the position you want it in while you load your jars.

After the jars are loaded, carefully unhook the rack and lower it into the water. Add more water if necessary so that the water is two inches above the tops of the jars. Put the lid of the canner on and turn to high heat. When water begins a steady boil, lower the heat a little but maintain the boil. Start your timing now. (For example, if you're supposed to process the jars for 15 minutes, start timing once the water begins to boil.)

When the allotted time has passed, turn off the heat. Slowly lift the rack to the halfway position again and carefully remove the jars, one at a time. There are jar lifters available in stores for this.

ONCE YOU'RE DONE

Let the jars rest 24 hours. During this period never press down on the tops of jars to see if they are sealed.

After 24 hours, check the seals by pressing down on the tops. If the top is indented, that means the jar is sealed. If any jars did not seal or they popped down when you pressed the top, the jar did not seal properly; be sure to store these jars in the fridge and use the contents soon.

You can remove the rings from the jars that sealed, if you wish. Store in a cool place.

Homespun Pouches & Bags

Throughout this book you're encouraged to slip a gift mix into a homemade fabric bag—and here are the simple instructions:

FIND YOUR FABRIC

Select a piece of cloth that coordinates with your gift. For instance, a cheerful spring print shows off Carrot Cake Mix, or a fall-colored plaid fabric looks homey with Apple Spice Cake Mix. You'll need a $1/2$ yard, with leftovers. (Note: You can adjust the size for a larger or smaller pouch, as you tailor recipes for different folks.)

Cut two 8- by 12-inch rectangles out of your fabric.

STITCH AWAY

- Place the two pieces right sides together.
- Using a half-inch seam, sew down one long side, across the bottom, and up the other long side. You should have one short side open at the top.
- Turn the semi-finished bag right side out.
- Fold down the top 1 inch inside the bag.
- Sew a half-inch seam around the top. If you have cut your rectangles out with pinking shears, there's no need to turn down the top or sew this seam.

ADMIRE YOUR HANDIWORK

Slip your mix inside and tie the pouch shut with ribbon.

Jar Toppers

In five steps and about five minutes you can top a jar in a delightful way. Ready? Go!

1. Pick a fabric that coordinates with your mix or basket theme.
2. For a mix in a regular mouth jar, cut a 7-inch circle from your fabric. A slightly larger diameter will do fine for a wide-mouth jar.
3. Lay the circle over the top of the jar with the completed mix inside. Let the material drape over the top.
4. Secure the fabric circle first with a rubberband and then with a bow made of jute twine, raffia, or colorful ribbon. If you plan to include a gift tag, thread one bow end through the tag's punched hole and continue to tie your bow.
5. Now glue or tuck in any accents you wish. Some of our favorites are:

- a button
- a cinnamon stick
- a dried orange or apple slice
- a mini Christmas ornament

- a sprig of holly or evergreen
- a decorative butter spreader
- an antique teaspoon
- a wooden spoon

Homemade Stamps

Long before craft shops devoted whole sections to stamps, special inks, and embossing powders for card-making, creative people made their own stamps from a variety of things common to the kitchen, including spuds. That's right: potato stamps.

You can do this on your own or with kids for fun and with charming, one-of-a-kind results.

POTATO STAMPS

For this you'll need:

- old newspapers
- an assortment of firm potatoes in a variety of shapes and sizes

- cookie cutters or other patterns
- a sharp knife (keep this away from the kids, though!)
- tempera paints in a variety of colors
- plastic plates
- the paper you want to stamp (sheets for gift wrap or stock for card-making)

Cover your work surface with plenty of newspapers. Scrub clean the potatoes and cut them in half. Each half will become a stamp.

Use the cookie cutters to cut the shape for your stamp into each potato half. Press the cutter about $1/2$ inch into the flat side of the potato. Then cut around that outline, removing the excess potato so the shape extends from the potato about $1/2$ inch.

If using a pattern instead of a cookie cutter, simply trace the shape you want onto the potato and cut around it—again, removing the excess potato so the shape you want extends $1/2$ inch.

Dip the potato evenly into the paint and firmly press it onto the paper. You can repeat stamps until the color fades, then dip and stamp again.

Discard the potatoes when done.

STAMPS THAT CAN BE REUSED

You can also make stamps that can be reused from a variety of the following household materials:

- erasers
- cork board
- Styrofoam
- household sponges
- very thick felt

Cut a desired shape from any of these elements. (For instance, pencil top erasers can be notched easily to make flowers. Another idea is to draw letters on Styrofoam [but don't forget to reverse the shape you cut for the stamped letter to appear correctly], cut out the shape, and use it to stamp initials and monograms.)

Once you've carved or cut out your shape, attach the "stamp" to a woodblock. Two-inch dowel pieces make great stamp blocks; craft glue or a hot glue gun works best for securing the materials.

Now the stamps are ready to use by pressing each one onto an ink pad and then paper. To keep the stamps in use longer, wipe them off with a damp sponge after working in each color.

10

WRAP IT UP—WITH TAGS
AND LABELS

decorative tag can add a classy finishing touch to any gift. Whether you're artsy and want to make your own tag or would rather rely on one you can copy and snip, you'll find what you need here: more than 250 ready-made gift tags. You can copy these on light-colored stock paper, cut out the tag, and include it with many of the gift mixes and ideas detailed on previous pages. For most ideas, two different designs of the tag are given from which you may choose your favorite.

Quick ideas on how to beautify any tag:

- Use paper with interesting colors and textures
- Cut out the tags with decorative-edged scissors
- Color in accents with markers, pencils, water paints, or tempera paints
- Stamp designs on blank tags
- Add accents like a glued-on button or trim
- Punch two holes side by side at the top of the tag. Slip one end of a ribbon through one hole; the other end through the other hole and tie a bow on the front of the card.
- Using double-stick tape, secure the tag onto a darker, coordinating color of card stock. You could even use corrugated cardboard or cardboard covered with fabric or felt. With a decorative-edged scissors, cut around your gift tag about ¼ inch outside the line of your light-colored tag.
- You can laminate recipe tags at several stores like Office Depot or Staples and some libraries, or you can cover them with clear Con-Tact paper.

You can secure tags to your gifts in interesting ways: Punch a hole in the top or corner and thread the tag onto your bow. If your ribbon is too wide to fit through the hole, use a short length of thin floral wire inserted through the punched hole to secure the tag to a bow or basket handle.

BLACK BEAN SOUP

Soak beans overnight in enough water to cover (8 to 10 cups). Drain the beans, add 8 cups of water, and simmer for two hours. Sauté two stalks of chopped celery in oil. Add this with the spice packet to the soup. Add 3 cups chopped, cooked ham. Simmer another 1½ to 2 hours or until the beans are tender. Add 16 ounces sour cream before serving.

⋇ SPLIT PEA ⋇ SOUP

Place contents of mix in a large kettle with 10 cups of water. Simmer for 1½ hours. Add:

1   chopped carrot
1   chopped celery stalk
2   peeled and cubed potatoes
2   cups cooked and chopped ham

Simmer for 1½ to 2 more hours until tender.

CREAM OF POTATO SOUP

To serve: Place ½ cup of soup mix in a bowl and add ⅔ cup boiling water. Stir until smooth.

BLACK BEAN SOUP

Soak beans overnight in enough water to cover (8 to 10 cups). Drain the beans, add 8 cups of water, and simmer for two hours. Sauté two stalks of chopped celery in oil. Add this with the spice packet to the soup. Add 3 cups chopped, cooked ham. Simmer another 1½ to 2 hours or until the beans are tender. Add 16 ounces sour cream before serving.

Split Pea Soup

Place contents of mix in a large kettle with 10 cups of water. Simmer for 1½ hours. Add:

1   chopped carrot
1   chopped celery stalk
2   peeled and cubed potatoes
2   cups cooked and chopped ham

Simmer for 1½ to 2 more hours until tender.

Cream of Potato Soup

To serve: Place ½ cup of soup mix in a bowl and add ⅔ cup boiling water. Stir until smooth.

FRENCH MARKET SOUP

Soak 4 cups of mix overnight in enough water to cover (12 to 14 cups). In the morning, cook over medium heat in a large kettle until slightly tender, about 2 hours. Add:

- 1 teaspoon chopped garlic
- 1 28-ounce can chopped tomatoes
- 3 cups chopped ham
- 1 chopped onion
- 1 tablespoon basil
- 1 teaspoon salt
- 1 sliced carrot

Continue cooking until tender, about 1½ hours.

Homemade PIZZA

- 2½ cups Handy Bread Mix
- 1 cup warm water
- 1 package or 2½ teaspoons yeast

Dissolve yeast in water. Let stand 10 minutes. Add Handy Bread Mix and blend well. Place in a well-greased bowl. Cover and let rise until doubled, about 1½ hours. Punch down and spread on a greased pizza pan or cookie sheet. Bake in a 425 degree oven for 5 minutes. Remove from oven. Spread with pizza sauce and your favorite toppings. Return to oven and bake 10 more minutes or until cheese is bubbly.

ITALIAN Breadsticks

- 2½ cups Handy Bread Mix
- 1 cup warm water
- 1 package or 2½ teaspoons yeast

Dissolve yeast in water. Let stand 10 minutes. Add Handy Bread Mix and blend well. Place in a well-greased bowl. Cover and let rise until doubled, about 1½ hours. Spread dough on a greased cookie sheet that has been lightly sprinkled with cornmeal. Cover with a clean towel and let rise for 45 minutes. With a sharp serrated knife, score into breadsticks of desired width. Brush the top lightly with 3 tablespoons melted butter. Sprinkle with a mixture of ¼ cup Parmesan cheese, 1 teaspoon basil, 1 teaspoon garlic powder, ½ teaspoon oregano, and ½ teaspoon salt. Bake at 400 degrees for 10 to 15 minutes or until lightly browned.

French Market SOUP

Soak 4 cups of mix overnight in enough water to cover (12 to 14 cups). In the morning, cook over medium heat in a large kettle until slightly tender, about 2 hours. Add:

- 1 teaspoon chopped garlic
- 1 28-ounce can chopped tomatoes
- 3 cups chopped ham
- 1 chopped onion
- 1 tablespoon basil
- 1 teaspoon salt
- 1 sliced carrot

Continue cooking until tender, about 1½ hours.

Homemade PIZZA

- 2½ cups Handy Bread Mix
- 1 cup warm water
- 1 package or 2½ teaspoons yeast

Dissolve yeast in water. Let stand 10 minutes. Add Handy Bread Mix and blend well. Place in a well-greased bowl. Cover and let rise until doubled, about 1½ hours. Punch down and spread on a greased pizza pan or cookie sheet. Bake in a 425 degree oven for 5 minutes. Remove from oven. Spread with pizza sauce and your favorite toppings. Return to oven and bake 10 more minutes or until cheese is bubbly.

Italian Breadsticks

- 2½ cups Handy Bread Mix
- 1 cup warm water
- 1 package or 2½ teaspoons yeast

Dissolve yeast in water. Let stand 10 minutes. Add Handy Bread Mix and blend well. Place in a well-greased bowl. Cover and let rise until doubled, about 1½ hours. Spread dough on a greased cookie sheet that has been lightly sprinkled with cornmeal. Cover with a clean towel and let rise for 45 minutes. With a sharp serrated knife, score into breadsticks of desired width. Brush the top lightly with 3 tablespoons melted butter. Sprinkle with a mixture of ¼ cup Parmesan cheese, 1 teaspoon basil, 1 teaspoon garlic powder, ½ teaspoon oregano, and ½ teaspoon salt. Bake at 400 degrees for 10 to 15 minutes or until lightly browned.

fresh Strawberry »Bread«

3 cups strawberries, fresh or frozen
1¼ cups oil
4 eggs, beaten

Mash and drain the strawberries, reserving half a cup of juice from berries. In a large bowl blend Fresh Strawberry Bread Mix, the berries, juice, oil, and eggs. Mix well. Pour into two greased loaf pans. Bake at 350 degrees 50 to 60 minutes. Cool completely before serving.

Apple Cinnamon Swirl BREAD

2½ cups Handy Bread Mix
¼ to ½ cup all-purpose flour
1 cup milk
2 tablespoons butter or margarine
1 package or 2½ teaspoons yeast
¼ cup sugar
1 teaspoon cinnamon
1 medium apple—cored, peeled, and chopped

Heat milk and butter until warm but not boiling. Remove from heat, stir in yeast, and let stand 10 minutes. Add Handy Bread Mix and blend well. Turn dough out onto a floured surface. Knead for 4 to 5 minutes, adding ¼ to ½ cup flour as needed to make a soft, but not sticky, dough. Roll out into a rectangle 15 by 7 inches. Mix sugar, cinnamon, and apples in a small bowl. Sprinkle mixture on top of the rectangle. Starting with the short side, roll the dough until you reach the other side. Wet edge with water and seal dough. Place in a greased loaf pan, seam side down. Cover and let rise for 45 minutes or until double. Bake in a 350 degree oven for 35 to 40 minutes. Allow bread to cool for 10 minutes. While cooling, combine ½ cup powdered sugar, 1 tablespoon milk, and ¼ teaspoon vanilla to form a glaze. Drizzle glaze over cooled bread.

F R E S H STRAWBERRY BREAD

3 cups strawberries, fresh or frozen
1¼ cups oil
4 eggs, beaten

Mash and drain the strawberries, reserving half a cup of juice from berries. In a large bowl blend Fresh Strawberry Bread Mix, the berries, juice, oil, and eggs. Mix well. Pour into two greased loaf pans. Bake at 350 degrees 50 to 60 minutes. Cool completely before serving.

Apple Cinnamon Swirl BREAD

2½ cups Handy Bread Mix
¼ to ½ cup all-purpose flour
1 cup milk
2 tablespoons butter or margarine
1 package or 2½ teaspoons yeast
¼ cup sugar
1 teaspoon cinnamon
1 medium apple—cored, peeled, and chopped

Heat milk and butter until warm but not boiling. Remove from heat, stir in yeast, and let stand 10 minutes. Add Handy Bread Mix and blend well. Turn dough out onto a floured surface. Knead for 4 to 5 minutes, adding ¼ to ½ cup flour as needed to make a soft, but not sticky, dough. Roll out into a rectangle 15 by 7 inches. Mix sugar, cinnamon, and apples in a small bowl. Sprinkle mixture on top of the rectangle. Starting with the short side, roll the dough until you reach the other side. Wet edge with water and seal dough. Place in a greased loaf pan, seam side down. Cover and let rise for 45 minutes or until double. Bake in a 350 degree oven for 35 to 40 minutes. Allow bread to cool for 10 minutes. While cooling, combine ½ cup powdered sugar, 1 tablespoon milk, and ¼ teaspoon vanilla to form a glaze. Drizzle glaze over cooled bread.

Chocolate Raspberry Swirl
B R E A D

❖ ❖ ❖ ❖

2½ cups Handy Bread Mix
¼ to ½ cup all-purpose flour
1 cup milk
2 tablespoons butter or margarine
1 package or 2½ teaspoons yeast
½ cup seedless raspberry jam
⅓ cup mini-chocolate chips

Heat milk and butter until warm but not boiling. Remove from heat, stir in yeast, and let stand 10 minutes. Add Handy Bread Mix and blend well. Turn dough out onto a floured surface. Knead for 4 to 5 minutes, adding ¼ to ½ cup flour as needed to make a soft, but not sticky, dough. Roll out into a rectangle 15 by 7 inches. Spread the raspberry jam on top of the rectangle. Sprinkle with mini-chocolate chips. Starting with the short side, roll the dough until you reach the other side. Wet edge with water and seal dough. Place in a greased loaf pan, seam side down. Cover and let rise for 45 minutes or until double. Bake in a 350 degree oven for 35 to 40 minutes. Allow bread to cool for 10 minutes. While cooling, combine ½ cup powdered sugar, 1 tablespoon milk, and ¼ teaspoon vanilla to form a glaze. Drizzle glaze over cooled bread.

Cakelike
C O R N   B R E A D

Combine in a large bowl:

1 package of Cakelike Corn Bread Mix
2 eggs
1 cup milk
½ cup melted butter

Pour batter into a greased 9- by 13-inch pan. Bake at 350 degrees for 30 minutes.

Chocolate Raspberry Swirl
B R E A D

2½ cups Handy Bread Mix
¼ to ½ cup all-purpose flour
1 cup milk
2 tablespoons butter or margarine
1 package or 2½ teaspoons yeast
½ cup seedless raspberry jam
⅓ cup mini-chocolate chips

Heat milk and butter until warm but not boiling. Remove from heat, stir in yeast, and let stand 10 minutes. Add Handy Bread Mix and blend well. Turn dough out onto a floured surface. Knead for 4 to 5 minutes, adding ¼ to ½ cup flour as needed to make a soft, but not sticky, dough. Roll out into a rectangle 15 by 7 inches. Spread the raspberry jam on top of the rectangle. Sprinkle with mini-chocolate chips. Starting with the short side, roll the dough until you reach the other side. Wet edge with water and seal dough. Place in a greased loaf pan, seam side down. Cover and let rise for 45 minutes or until double. Bake in a 350 degree oven for 35 to 40 minutes. Allow bread to cool for 10 minutes. While cooling, combine ½ cup powdered sugar, 1 tablespoon milk, and ¼ teaspoon vanilla to form a glaze. Drizzle glaze over cooled bread.

Cakelike
C O R N   B R E A D

Combine in a large bowl:

1 package of Cakelike Corn Bread Mix
2 eggs
1 cup milk
½ cup melted butter

Pour batter into a greased 9- by 13-inch pan. Bake at 350 degrees for 30 minutes.

FIVE-FRUIT
Bread

In a bowl, mix one 15-ounce can of fruit cocktail, including juice, with this bread mix. Add 1 teaspoon vanilla. Pour into 8-inch square pan. Mix the sugar and coconut topping ingredients well and sprinkle on top. Bake for 40 to 45 minutes at 350 degrees. Cool slightly and serve with whipped cream or ice cream.

Five-Fruit
BREAD

In a bowl, mix one 15-ounce can of fruit cocktail, including juice, with this bread mix. Add 1 teaspoon vanilla. Pour into 8-inch square pan. Mix the sugar and coconut topping ingredients well and sprinkle on top. Bake for 40 to 45 minutes at 350 degrees. Cool slightly and serve with whipped cream or ice cream.

HARVEST PUMPKIN *muffins*

Place all jar contents (except the bagged topping) into a large bowl and mix. In a smaller bowl beat:

1   egg
½   cup milk
½   cup canned pumpkin
¼   cup vegetable oil

Pour the egg mixture into the dry ingredients, and stir only until combined. Fill lightly greased muffin cups two-thirds full. Sprinkle with sugar and cinnamon topping. Bake in a preheated, 400 degree oven for 20 minutes or until brown. Makes 12 delicious muffins.

HARVEST PUMPKIN **bread**

Place all jar contents (except the bagged topping) into a large bowl and mix. In a smaller bowl beat:

1   egg
½   cup milk
½   cup canned pumpkin
¼   cup vegetable oil

Pour the egg mixture into the dry ingredients, and stir only until combined. Pour this into a lightly greased loaf pan. Sprinkle with sugar and cinnamon topping. Bake in a preheated 350 degree oven for one hour. Makes one tasty loaf.

Ginger Spice MUFFINS

1   pkg Ginger Spice Muffin Mix
¼   cup melted butter
1   egg
1   teaspoon vanilla
1   cup milk

Combine this mix with all ingredients in a large bowl. Stir until just combined. Fill greased muffin tins two-thirds full. Bake at 400 degrees for 15 minutes. Makes a dozen.

HARVEST PUMPKIN *MUFFINS*

Place all jar contents (except the bagged topping) into a large bowl and mix. In a smaller bowl beat:

1   egg
½   cup milk
½   cup canned pumpkin
¼   cup vegetable oil

Pour the egg mixture into the dry ingredients, and stir only until combined. Fill lightly greased muffin cups two-thirds full. Sprinkle with sugar and cinnamon topping. Bake in a preheated, 400 degree oven for 20 minutes or until brown. Makes 12 delicious muffins.

HARVEST PUMPKIN **BREAD**

Place all jar contents (except the bagged topping) into a large bowl and mix. In a smaller bowl beat:

1   egg
½   cup milk
½   cup canned pumpkin
¼   cup vegetable oil

Pour the egg mixture into the dry ingredients, and stir only until combined. Pour this into a lightly greased loaf pan. Sprinkle with sugar and cinnamon topping. Bake in a preheated 350 degree oven for one hour. Makes one tasty loaf.

Ginger Spice MUFFINS

1   pkg Ginger Spice Muffin Mix
¼   cup melted butter
1   egg
1   teaspoon vanilla
1   cup milk

Combine this mix with all ingredients in a large bowl. Stir until just combined. Fill greased muffin tins two-thirds full. Bake at 400 degrees for 15 minutes. Makes a dozen.

CHOCOLATE CHIP
Muffins

In a large bowl mix:

⅔ cup milk
½ cup melted butter,
   slightly cooled
1 teaspoon vanilla
2 beaten eggs

Add this Chocolate Chip Muffin Mix and stir just until blended. Pour into greased muffin cups. Bake at 375 degrees for 20 to 25 minutes.

COFFEE CAKE
MUFFINS

¼ cup shortening
1 beaten egg
½ cup milk
1 tablespoon melted butter

Place the flour mixture into a large bowl. Cut in the shortening. In a small bowl, mix egg and milk. Combine egg and flour mixtures, stirring just until combined. In another bowl, mix the cinnamon mixture with the melted butter. Fill greased muffin tins two-thirds full. Sprinkle with cinnamon mixture. Bake at 350 degrees for 20 minutes.

Lemon Poppy Seed
✦ MUFFINS ✦

Mix 1 package of Lemon Poppy Seed Muffin Mix with:

¼ cup vegetable oil
¼ cup water
1⅓ cups sour cream
2 eggs
⅓ cup lemon juice
1 teaspoon almond extract
   (optional)

Pour into greased and floured muffin tins and bake at 375 degrees for 15 to 20 minutes or until a toothpick inserted comes out clean. Cool 10 minutes. Remove and cool completely.

Chocolate Chip
Muffins

In a large bowl mix:

⅔ cup milk
½ cup melted butter,
   slightly cooled
1 teaspoon vanilla
2 beaten eggs

Add this Chocolate Chip Muffin Mix and stir just until blended. Pour into greased muffin cups. Bake at 375 degrees for 20 to 25 minutes.

COFFEE CAKE
MUFFINS

¼ cup shortening
1 beaten egg
½ cup milk
1 tablespoon melted butter

Place the flour mixture into a large bowl. Cut in the shortening. In a small bowl, mix egg and milk. Combine egg and flour mixtures, stirring just until combined. In another bowl, mix the cinnamon mixture with the melted butter. Fill greased muffin tins two-thirds full. Sprinkle with cinnamon mixture. Bake at 350 degrees for 20 minutes.

Lemon Poppy Seed
MUFFINS

Mix 1 package of Lemon Poppy Seed Muffin Mix with:

¼ cup vegetable oil
¼ cup water
1⅓ cups sour cream
2 eggs
⅓ cup lemon juice
1 teaspoon almond extract
   (optional)

Pour into greased and floured muffin tins and bake at 375 degrees for 15 to 20 minutes or until a toothpick inserted comes out clean. Cool 10 minutes. Remove and cool completely.

SPICE CAKE

Combine Apple Spice Cake Mix with:

1½ cups vegetable oil
3 large eggs
1 teaspoon vanilla
3 cups chopped apples

Stir until smooth. Spread batter into a lightly greased and floured 9 x 13-inch pan. Bake at 350 degrees for 45 minutes.

Apple
SPICE CAKE

Combine Apple Spice Cake Mix with:

1½ cups vegetable oil
3 large eggs
1 teaspoon vanilla
3 cups chopped apples

Stir until smooth. Spread batter into a lightly greased and floured 9 x 13-inch pan. Bake at 350 degrees for 45 minutes.

Tag-errific

Photocopy the tag to the right onto an 8½- by 11-inch piece of parchment-type card stock and cut out. With pinking shears, cut a piece of burgundy plaid fabric 3½ inches wide by 12 inches long. Wrap the fabric around the middle of a quart jar lengthwise, securing with double-stick tape. Now wrap the instructional tag around the middle, centering it on the fabric and the front of the jar. Secure at the back with double-stick tape.

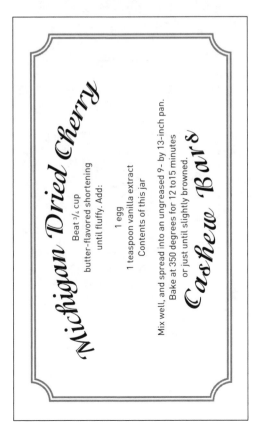

Michigan Dried Cherry Cashew Bars

Beat ¾ cup butter-flavored shortening until fluffy. Add:

1 egg
1 teaspoon vanilla extract
Contents of this jar

Mix well, and spread into an ungreased 9- by 13-inch pan. Bake at 350 degrees for 12 to15 minutes or just until slightly browned.

MICHIGAN DRIED CHERRY CASHEW BARS

Beat ¾ cup butter-flavored shortening until fluffy. Add:

1 egg
1 teaspoon vanilla extract
Contents of this jar

Mix well, and spread into an ungreased 9- by 13-inch pan. Bake at 350 degrees for 12 to15 minutes or just until slightly browned.

PEANUT BUTTER ⚔ CHIP ⚔
Cookies

In a large bowl, beat:

¾ cup butter
1 egg
1 teaspoon vanilla

Mix in all ingredients from this jar. Drop the dough by spoonfuls onto a slightly greased cookie sheet. Bake 8 to 10 minutes at 375 degrees.

family favorite
SUGAR COOKIES

Cream together 2 cups each of butter and sugar. Blend in 2 eggs and 4 teaspoons vanilla extract. Add this mix and blend.

Cover and refrigerate 4 balls of dough at least 4 hours. Roll out on a floured surface and cut with cookie cutters. Bake at 350 degrees for 8 to 10 minutes.

OATMEAL
COCONUT
CRUNCHIES

Cream together:

½ cup butter
½ tablespoon milk
2 teaspoons vanilla
1 egg

Add the ingredients from this jar, mixing well. Bake at 375 degrees for 9 to 13 minutes on an ungreased cookie sheet. This recipe makes 2 dozen cookies.

PEANUT BUTTER CHIP
Cookies

In a large bowl, beat:

¾ cup butter
1 egg
1 teaspoon vanilla

Mix in all ingredients from this jar. Drop the dough by spoonfuls onto a slightly greased cookie sheet. Bake 8 to 10 minutes at 375 degrees.

family favorite
Sugar Cookies

Cream together 2 cups each of butter and sugar. Blend in 2 eggs and 4 teaspoons vanilla extract. Add this mix and blend.

Cover and refrigerate 4 balls of dough at least 4 hours. Roll out on a floured surface and cut with cookie cutters. Bake at 350 degrees for 8 to 10 minutes.

OATMEAL
Coconut Crunchies

Cream together:

½ cup butter
½ tablespoon milk
2 teaspoons vanilla
1 egg

Add the ingredients from this jar, mixing well. Bake at 375 degrees for 9 to 13 minutes on an ungreased cookie sheet. This recipe makes 2 dozen cookies.

COWBOY COOKIES

Beat together:

1 cup butter until fluffy
2 eggs
1 teaspoon vanilla

Stir in the ingredients in this mix, until well blended. With a ¼ cup measure, scoop cookie dough onto an ungreased baking sheet. Use a wet glass to press each cookie and flatten it. Bake at 350 degrees for 13 to 15 minutes.

➤ VERY BERRY ➤
COBBLER

Preheat the oven to 375 degrees, and mix:

1 quart fresh blueberries, blackberries, or raspberries
¼ cup orange juice
¼ cup sugar
1 teaspoon cinnamon

Place fruit mixture in a greased 9- by 13-inch pan. Right into this bag of cobbler mix, add 1 egg and 1 cup melted butter. Seal and knead to combine. Drop the cobbler mixture by spoonfuls onto the berries. Bake for 35 to 40 minutes. Let cool before serving.

CARROT CAKE

Blend Carrot Cake Mix with:

1½ cups vegetable oil
1 8-ounce can crushed pineapple, undrained
3 large eggs
1 teaspoon vanilla
3 cups grated carrots

Stir until smooth. Pour into greased 9- by 13-inch pan. Bake at 350 degrees for 40 to 50 minutes. Cool the cake completely and frost if desired.

COWBOY COOKIES

Beat together:

1 cup butter until fluffy
2 eggs
1 teaspoon vanilla

Stir in the ingredients in this mix, until well blended. With a ¼ cup measure, scoop cookie dough onto an ungreased baking sheet. Use a wet glass to press each cookie and flatten it. Bake at 350 degrees for 13 to 15 minutes.

VERY BERRY COBBLER

Preheat the oven to 375 degrees, and mix:

1 quart fresh blueberries, blackberries, or raspberries
¼ cup orange juice
¼ cup sugar
1 teaspoon cinnamon

Place fruit mixture in a greased 9- by 13-inch pan. Right into this bag of cobbler mix, add 1 egg and 1 cup melted butter. Seal and knead to combine. Drop the cobbler mixture by spoonfuls onto the berries. Bake for 35 to 40 minutes. Let cool before serving.

Carrot Cake

Blend Carrot Cake Mix with:

1½ cups vegetable oil
1 8-ounce can crushed pineapple, undrained
3 large eggs
1 teaspoon vanilla
3 cups grated carrots

Stir until smooth. Pour into greased 9- by 13-inch pan. Bake at 350 degrees for 40 to 50 minutes. Cool the cake completely and frost if desired.

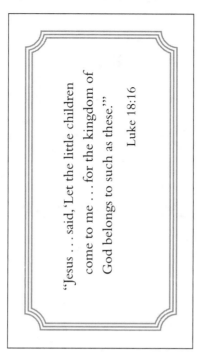

"Jesus . . . said, 'Let the little children come to me . . . for the kingdom of God belongs to such as these.'"

Luke 18:16

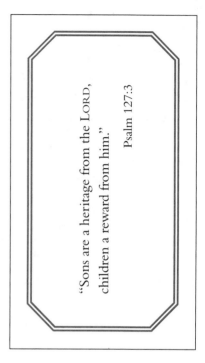

"Sons are a heritage from the LORD, children a reward from him."

Psalm 127:3

"Jesus . . . said,
'Let the little
children come
to me . . .
for the kingdom
of God belongs
to such as these.'"

Luke 18:16

"Sons are
a heritage
from
the LORD,
children
a reward
from him."

Psalm 127:3

"He who finds a wife finds what is good and receives favor from the LORD."
Proverbs 18:22

"But as for me and my household, we will serve the LORD."
Joshua 24:15

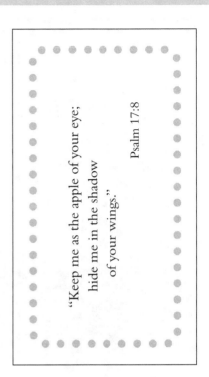
"Keep me as the apple of your eye; hide me in the shadow of your wings."
Psalm 17:8

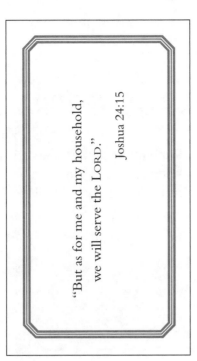
"He who finds a wife finds what is good and receives favor from the LORD."
Proverbs 18:22

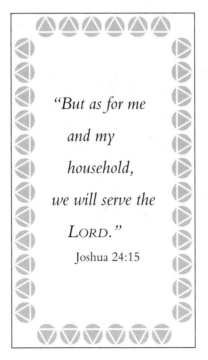
"But as for me and my household, we will serve the LORD."
Joshua 24:15

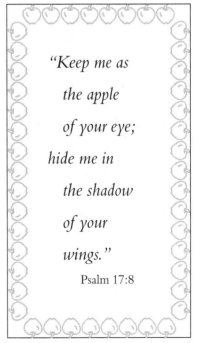
"Keep me as the apple of your eye; hide me in the shadow of your wings."
Psalm 17:8

ORANGE
Cappuccino

Per cup: Spoon 3 table-spoons of mix into a mug. Add 1 cup of boil-ing water and stir.

MOCHA
Cappuccino

Per cup: Spoon 3 table-spoons of mix into a mug. Add 1 cup of boil-ing water and stir.

CINNAMON
Cappuccino

Per cup: Spoon 3 table-spoons of mix into a mug. Add 1 cup of boil-ing water and stir.

ORANGE
Cappuccino

Per cup: Spoon 3 tablespoons of mix into a mug. Add 1 cup of boiling water and stir.

MOCHA
Cappuccino

Per cup: Spoon 3 tablespoons of mix into a mug. Add 1 cup of boiling water and stir.

CINNAMON
Cappuccino

Per cup: Spoon 3 tablespoons of mix into a mug. Add 1 cup of boiling water and stir.

CHOCOLATE MINT
Coffee

Per cup: Spoon 3 tablespoons of mix into a mug. Add 1 cup of boiling water and stir.

RICH & CREAMY
Hot Chocolate

Per cup: Spoon $1/4$ cup of mix into a mug. Add 1 cup of boiling water and stir until dissolved. For an extra special treat, top with mini-marshmallows.

MEXICAN HOT
Chocolate

Boil 3 cups water. Add the Mexican Hot Chocolate mix along with 1½ teaspoons vanilla. Stir with a whisk until smooth and creamy. Enjoy this with a friend.

Chocolate Mint
Coffee

Per cup: Spoon 3 tablespoons of mix into a mug. Add 1 cup of boiling water and stir.

Rich & Creamy Hot Chocolate

Per cup: Spoon $1/4$ cup of mix into a mug. Add 1 cup of boiling water and stir until dissolved. For an extra special treat, top with mini-marshmallows.

MEXICAN
HOT
Chocolate

Boil 3 cups water. Add the Mexican Hot Chocolate mix along with 1½ teaspoons vanilla. Stir with a whisk until smooth and creamy. Enjoy this with a friend.

WHITE HOT
Chocolate

In a small saucepan, heat $1^1/_2$ cups milk until hot. Add $^1/_4$ cup White Hot Chocolate mix and $^1/_2$ teaspoon vanilla and whisk until the chocolate is melted. Continue to whisk until the mixture is hot.

HAPPY WINTER

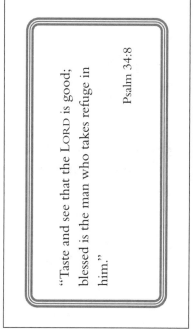

"Taste and see that the LORD is good; blessed is the man who takes refuge in him."

Psalm 34:8

WHITE HOT
CHOCOLATE

In a small saucepan, heat $1^1/_2$ cups milk until hot. Add $^1/_4$ cup White Hot Chocolate mix and $^1/_2$ teaspoon vanilla and whisk until the chocolate is melted. Continue to whisk until the mixture is hot.

Happy
Winter

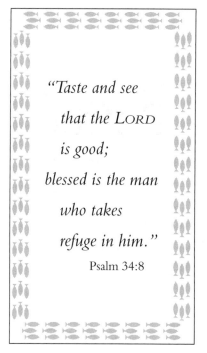

"Taste and see that the LORD is good; blessed is the man who takes refuge in him."

Psalm 34:8

YE OLDE SNOWMAN IN A BOX KIT

"The fruit of
righteousness
is a tree of life,
and he who wins souls
is wise."

Proverbs 11:30

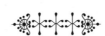

"Wash me,
and I will be whiter than snow."

Psalm 51:7

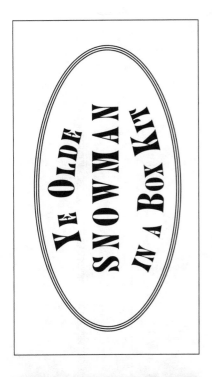

YE OLDE
SNOWMAN
IN A BOX
KIT

Proverbs 11:30

"The fruit of righteousness
is a tree of life,
and he who wins souls
is wise."

"Wash me,
and I will be
whiter
than snow."

Psalm 51:7

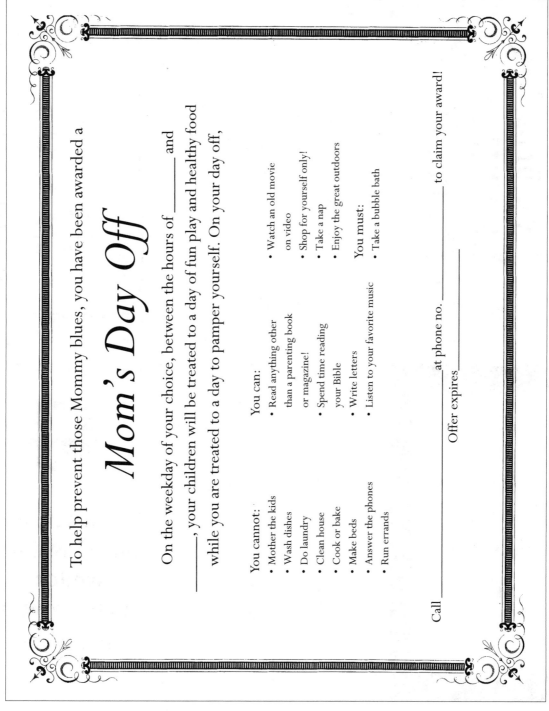

To help prevent those Mommy blues, you have been awarded a

Mom's Day Off

On the weekday of your choice, between the hours of _____ and _____, your children will be treated to a day of fun play and healthy food while you are treated to a day to pamper yourself. On your day off,

You cannot:
- Mother the kids
- Wash dishes
- Do laundry
- Clean house
- Cook or bake
- Make beds
- Answer the phones
- Run errands

You can:
- Read anything other than a parenting book or magazine!
- Spend time reading your Bible
- Write letters
- Listen to your favorite music
- Watch an old movie on video
- Shop for yourself only!
- Take a nap
- Enjoy the great outdoors

You must:
- Take a bubble bath

Call _____ at phone no. _____ to claim your award!

Offer expires _____

Italian MARINADE

¼ cup of this spice mix
½ cup olive oil
⅔ cup red wine vinegar
½ cup water

Mix ingredients well. Use this marinade on chicken, beef, or vegetables overnight, and grill to your finger-licking liking.

CAJUN SEASONING

Use this tangy seasoning on chicken, fish, beef, or vegetables.

Lemon Pepper SEASONING

2 teaspoons of this mix
¼ cup fresh lemon juice
¼ cup olive oil

Mix ingredients well. Place 1 pound of boneless, skinless chicken breast in this marinade for 30 minutes, and grill as desired.

Italian Marinade

¼ cup of this spice mix
½ cup olive oil
⅔ cup red wine vinegar
½ cup water

Mix ingredients well. Use this marinade on chicken, beef, or vegetables overnight, and grill to your finger-licking liking.

CAJUN SEASONING

Use this tangy seasoning on chicken, fish, beef, or vegetables.

LEMON PEPPER SEASONING

2 teaspoons of this mix
¼ cup fresh lemon juice
¼ cup olive oil

Mix ingredients well. Place 1 pound of boneless, skinless chicken breast in this marinade for 30 minutes, and grill as desired.

OVEN FRIED chicken

Dip 2 pounds of chicken pieces into a bowl of milk and then into $2/3$ cup of this coating. Place the chicken in an ungreased baking pan, and bake at 400 degrees for 50 to 60 minutes or until golden brown.

Country DILL DIP

4 tablespoons Country Dill Dip Mix
1 cup sour cream
1 cup salad dressing

Mix ingredients well. Chill for two hours before serving.

OVEN FRIED CHICKEN

Dip 2 pounds of chicken pieces into a bowl of milk and then into $2/3$ cup of this coating. Place the chicken in an ungreased baking pan, and bake at 400 degrees for 50 to 60 minutes or until golden brown.

COUNTRY DILL DIP

4 tablespoons Country Dill Dip Mix
1 cup sour cream
1 cup salad dressing

Mix ingredients well. Chill for two hours before serving.

southwestern

VEGGIE DIP

3 tablespoons South-
western Veggie Dip
Mix

1 cup mayonnaise

1 cup sour cream

Mix ingredients well. Chill
for two hours. Serve with
tortilla chips or fresh veggies.

---

*When you lie
down,
you will not be
afraid;
when you lie
down, your sleep
will be sweet.*

Proverbs 3:24

CREAMY RANCH DRESSING OR DIP

FOR DRESSING

2 tablespoons Creamy Ranch
Dressing or Dip Mix

1 cup mayonnaise

1 cup buttermilk

Mix ingredients well. Keep refrigerated.

FOR DIP

2 tablespoons Creamy Ranch
Dressing or Dip Mix

1 cup mayonnaise

1 cup sour cream

Mix ingredients well.

Keep refrigerated.

Southwestern Veggie Dip

3 tablespoons South-
western Veggie Dip
Mix

1 cup mayonnaise

1 cup sour cream

Mix ingredients well. Chill
for two hours. Serve with tortilla chips or fresh veggies.

---

*When you lie down,
you will not be afraid;
when you lie down,
your sleep will be sweet.*

Proverbs 3:24

❧ CALICO ❧
Baked Beans

8-ounce can tomato sauce
2   cups ketchup
1   thinly sliced onion
1   thinly sliced green pepper
½   pound cooked and crumbled bacon

Cover the beans with water and soak overnight. Drain. Place in a large pot and add 10 to 12 cups of water. Cook over medium-low heat until tender, about 3 hours. Drain. Mix in the bacon, onion, and pepper; place in large oven-proof casserole dish.

In a medium bowl, mix the spice packet with the tomato sauce and ketchup. Pour this over the bean mixture and mix well. Add a bit more ketchup if needed. Mixture should seem slightly soupy. Bake at 350 degrees for 1 to 1½ hours.

Mother-in-Law
REFRIGERATOR
PICKLES

Calico
BAKED BEANS

8-ounce can tomato sauce
2   cups ketchup
1   thinly sliced onion
1   thinly sliced green pepper
½   pound cooked and crumbled bacon

Cover the beans with water and soak overnight. Drain. Place in a large pot and add 10 to 12 cups of water. Cook over medium-low heat until tender, about 3 hours. Drain. Mix in the bacon, onion, and pepper; place in large oven-proof casserole dish.

In a medium bowl, mix the spice packet with the tomato sauce and ketchup. Pour this over the bean mixture and mix well. Add a bit more ketchup if needed. Mixture should seem slightly soupy. Bake at 350 degrees for 1 to 1½ hours.

MOTHER-IN-LAW REFRIGERATOR PICKLES

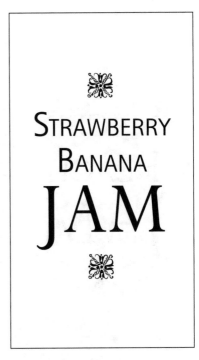

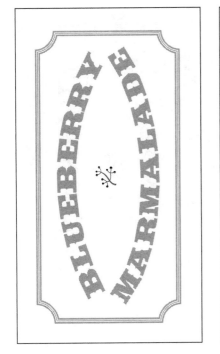

SPICED PEACH JAM

> "A new command I give to you: Love one another. As I have loved you, so you must love one another."
>
> John 13:34

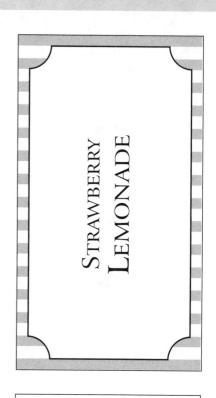

STRAWBERRY LEMONADE

SPICED PEACH JAM

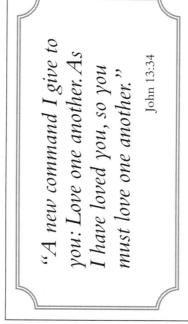

> "A new command I give to you: Love one another. As I have loved you, so you must love one another."
>
> John 13:34

STRAWBERRY LEMONADE

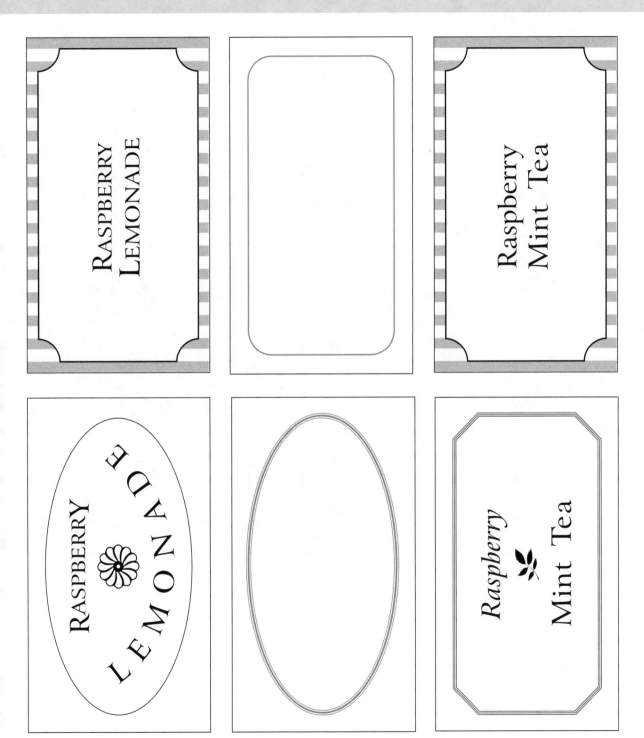

RASPBERRY LEMONADE

Raspberry Mint Tea

RASPBERRY LEMONADE

Raspberry Mint Tea

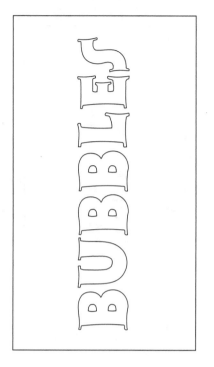

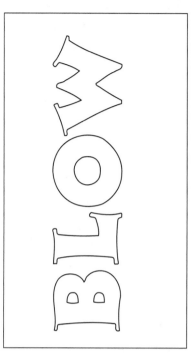

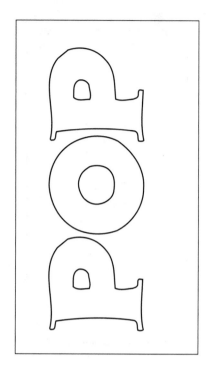

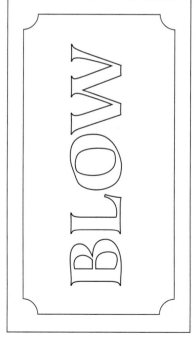

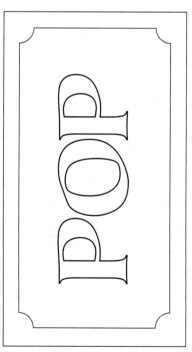

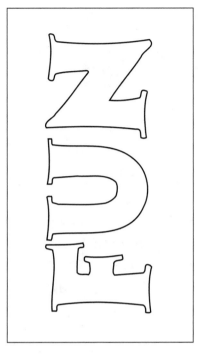

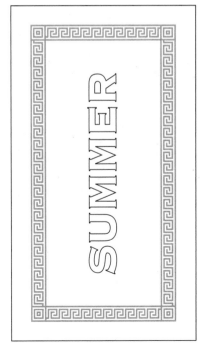

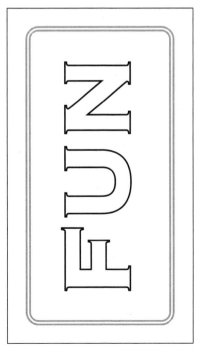

HAPPY
FOURTH
of
JULY!

"Though your sins
are like scarlet,
they shall be as
white as snow;
though they are
red as crimson,
they shall be
like wool."

Isaiah 1:18

"I am the vine;
you are the
branches. If a man
remains in me and
I in him, he will
bear much fruit;
apart from me you
can do nothing."

John 15:5

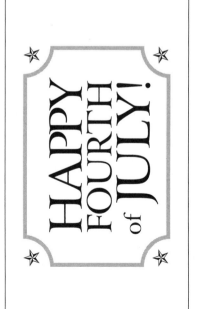

*"Though your sins are like scarlet,
they shall be as white as snow;
though they are red as crimson,
they shall be like wool."*

Isaiah 1:18

*"I am the vine; you are the branches.
If a man remains in me and I in him,
he will bear much fruit; apart from me
you can do nothing."*

John 15:5

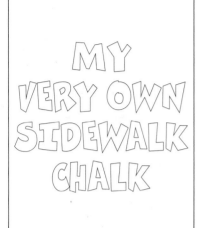

MY VERY OWN SIDEWALK CHALK

"But the fruit of the Spirit is love, joy, peace, patience, kindness, goodness, faithfulness, gentleness and self-control. Against such things there is no law."

Galatians 5:22–23

MY VERY OWN SIDEWALK CHALK

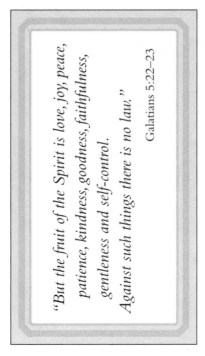

"But the fruit of the Spirit is love, joy, peace, patience, kindness, goodness, faithfulness, gentleness and self-control. Against such things there is no law."

Galatians 5:22–23

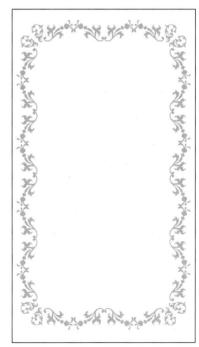

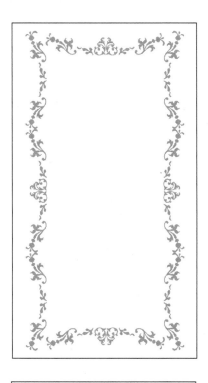

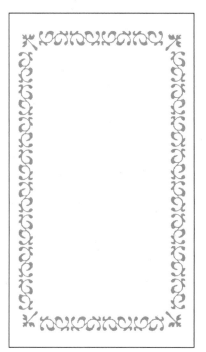

HOMEMADE
DOG
TREATS

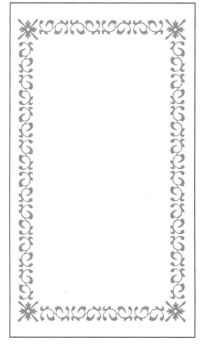

PEOPLE

CHOW

• FOR THE •

MASTER

People Chow for the Master

READY-READER

ALPHABET

SOUP

1	bag frozen, mixed vegetables
28	oz. can diced tomatoes
8	cups water
1	pkg. Reader-Ready Alphabet Soup Mix

Simmer first three ingredients until mixed vegetables are tender, about ½ hour. Add mix. Continue simmering until pasta is done, about ½ hour longer.

READY-READER

1 bag frozen, mixed vegetables
28 oz. can diced tomatoes
8 cups water
1 pkg. Reader-Ready Alphabet Soup Mix

Simmer first three ingredients until mixed vegetables are tender, about ½ hour. Add mix. Continue simmering until pasta is done, about ½ hour longer.

ALPHABET SOUP

WHOLE WHEAT BREAD IN A BAG

Add to the large bag:

2   tablespoons canola oil
2   tablespoons honey
1   cup warm water

Squeeze out the air and reseal the bag. Squeeze the bag with your hands to mix the contents until smooth. Then open and add the little bag of flour. Reseal the bag, squeezing out the air. Knead the dough for 10 minutes. Then place the bag in a warm place, covered with a kitchen towel. Let rise until doubled, about 1 hour.

While the dough is rising, grease your loaf pan. When the dough is ready, punch down with your fists and then take it out of the bag. Put the dough into your bread pan. Cover with a clean dish towel and let rise until double again, about $1/2$ hour.

Bake at 350 degrees for 30 to 35 minutes or until golden brown. If the crust browns too quickly, cover loosely with a piece of foil.

"Give us today our daily bread."

Matthew 6:11

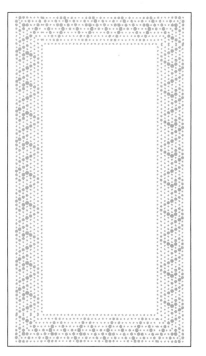

"Give us today our daily bread."

Matthew 6:11

Happy Reading!

"For the LORD
gives wisdom
and from his
mouth
come knowledge
and
understanding."

PROVERBS 2:6

WELCOME
 TO THE
NEIGHBORHOOD!

Don't hesitate to call for anything you need. Save this tag
and redeem it for one home-
cooked meal.

Neighborly yours,

_____

Phone number:

_____

"I pray that out of
his glorious riches
he may strengthen
you with power
through his Spirit
in your
inner being."

Ephesians 3:16

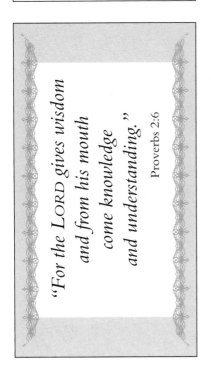

"For the LORD gives wisdom
and from his mouth
come knowledge
and understanding."

Proverbs 2:6

WELCOME
to the
Neighborhood!

Don't hesitate to call for anything you need.
Save this tag and redeem it for one home-
cooked meal.

Neighborly yours,

_____

Phone number:

_____

"I pray that out of his glorious
riches he may strengthen you
with power through his
Spirit in your inner being."

Ephesians 3:16

"How
beautiful
are the feet
of those
who bring
good news!"

Romans 10:15

"Jesus answered,
'I am the way
and the truth
and the life.
No one comes
to the Father
except
through me.'"

John 14:6

*"How beautiful are
the feet of those
who bring good news!"*

Romans 10:15

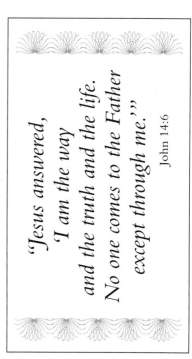

*"Jesus answered,
'I am the way
and the truth and the life.
No one comes to the Father
except through me.'"*

John 14:6

"As the deer
pants for streams
of water, so my
soul pants
for you, O
God."

PSALM 42:1

"Keep me
as the apple
of Your
eye."

PSALM 17:8
(NKJV)

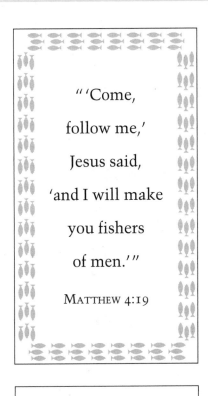

"'Come,
follow me,'
Jesus said,
'and I will make
you fishers
of men.'"

MATTHEW 4:19

"As the deer pants for streams of water,
so my soul pants for you, O God."

PSALM 42:1

"Keep me as
the apple of
Your eye."

PSALM 17:8
(NKJV)

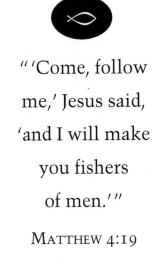

"'Come, follow
me,' Jesus said,
'and I will make
you fishers
of men.'"

MATTHEW 4:19

*For the
Beautiful Bride:*

- Something Old
- Something New
- Something Borrowed
- Something Blue
- Silver Sixpence
- God Loves You

*Homemade
Stationery Kit*

"*I am the vine;
you are the
branches. If a man
remains in me and
I in him, he will
bear much fruit;
apart from me you
can do nothing.*"

John 15:5

✳ ✳ ✳ ✳ ✳ ✳ ✳

*For the
Beautiful Bride:*

- Something Old
- Something New
- Something Borrowed
- Something Blue
- Silver Sixpence
- God Loves You

✳ ✳ ✳ ✳ ✳ ✳ ✳

*Homemade

Stationery

Kit*

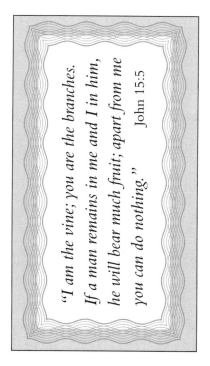

"*I am the vine; you are the branches.
If a man remains in me and I in him,
he will bear much fruit; apart from me
you can do nothing.*"   John 15:5

Homemade Spaghetti Sauce

1½ cups chopped onion
1 12-ounce can tomato paste
3 28-ounce cans crushed tomatoes
2 cups water
4 teaspoons minced garlic
4 bay leaves
4 teaspoons dried basil leaves, double if fresh
2 teaspoons dried oregano, double if fresh
3 tablespoons chopped fresh parsley
½ teaspoon thyme
2 teaspoons salt

In a large pot, stir together all the ingredients and bring to a boil. Reduce heat. Cover and simmer for 2 hours, stirring occasionally. Serve with your favorite pasta.

T·H·E Pizza Garden

Dig a circular plot in your yard or garden. With a hoe or sticks and string, divide the circle into "slices" like on a pie. In each slice plant one of these ingredients for a yummy pizza. When the vegetables and herbs are ready, have Mom or Dad help you make a pizza. Happy planting and eating!

If life hands you lemons, make lemonade.

HOMEMADE SPAGHETTI SAUCE

1½ cups chopped onion
1 12-ounce can tomato paste
3 28-ounce cans crushed tomatoes
2 cups water
4 teaspoons minced garlic
4 bay leaves
4 teaspoons dried basil leaves, double if fresh
2 teaspoons dried oregano, double if fresh
3 tablespoons chopped fresh parsley
½ teaspoon thyme
2 teaspoons salt

In a large pot, stir together all the ingredients and bring to a boil. Reduce heat. Cover and simmer for 2 hours, stirring occasionally. Serve with your favorite pasta.

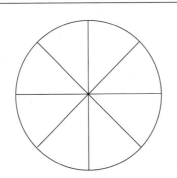

The Pizza Garden

Dig a circular plot in your yard or garden. With a hoe or sticks and string, divide the circle into "slices" like on a pie. In each slice plant one of these ingredients for a yummy pizza. When the vegetables and herbs are ready, have Mom or Dad help you make a pizza. Happy planting and eating!

If life hands you lemons, make lemonade.

169

Honey Mustard Dressing

1   cup mayonnaise
¼   cup honey
¼   cup Dijon mustard
2   tablespoons sugar
1   tablespoon parsley (optional)

Stir ingredients before serving. Store in refrigerator.

"I tell you the truth,
if you have faith
as small as a mustard seed,
you can say
to this mountain,
'Move from here to there'
and it will move.
Nothing will be impossible
for you."

Matthew 17:20

Blooms in a Bucket

You can force these amaryllis bulbs to bloom early in winter. Just add a little water to this container, and when a stalk begins to sprout, carefully remove the bulb. Drain any water (keeping pebbles in the bottom for more drainage), add potting soil, and water a bit each week until the bulb blooms.

"I tell you the truth, if you have faith as small as a mustard seed, you can say to this mountain, 'Move from here to there' and it will move. Nothing will be impossible for you."

Matthew 17:20

 ## HONEY MUSTARD DRESSING

1   cup mayonnaise
¼   cup honey
¼   cup Dijon mustard
2   tablespoons sugar
1   tablespoon parsley (optional)

Stir ingredients before serving. Store in refrigerator.

BLOOMS IN A BUCKET

You can force these amaryllis bulbs to bloom early in winter. Just add a little water to this container, and when a stalk begins to sprout, carefully remove the bulb. Drain any water (keeping pebbles in the bottom for more drainage), add potting soil, and water a bit each week until the bulb blooms.

Kitchen Herbs

"The seed on good soil stands for those with a noble and good heart, who hear the word, retain it, and by persevering produce a crop."

Luke 8:15

Follow directions on the seed packets to plant your very own Kitchen Herb Garden—a garden fit for a windowsill.

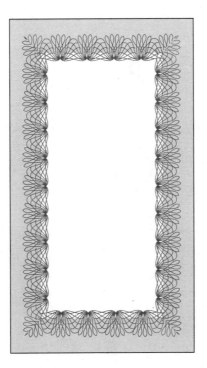

Scarecrow Kit

Each year when fall hits the air, pull me out and put me together. I'll keep you company and make your porch look cute. I may even scare away a crow or two!

Kitchen Herbs

"The seed on good soil stands for those with a noble and good heart, who hear the word, retain it, and by persevering produce a crop."

Luke 8:15

Follow directions on the seed packets to plant your very own Kitchen Herb Garden—a garden fit for a windowsill.

Scarecrow Kit

Each year when fall hits the air, pull me out and put me together. I'll keep you company and make your porch look cute. I may even scare away a crow or two!

SPICED

Apple Cider

Place this spice packet, still in its cheesecloth, in a large saucepan or slow cooker with:

2   quarts apple cider
1   quart water
1   orange, sliced

Heat until warm, but do not boil. Serve warm and sip a taste of something good!

REFRIGERATOR
Biscuit
Donuts

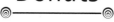

Open the biscuits. With the neck of an empty pop bottle, make a hole in the center of each biscuit. Remove the "hole." Heat 2 inches of oil over medium-high heat in a deep skillet. Place 4 to 5 biscuits in the oil and cook 1 to 2 minutes. Turn, cook 1 to 2 minutes more or until lightly browned. Remove. Place each donut in a bag of sugar and shake, coating well. Place on paper towels to cool.

APPLE
CIDER
DONUTS

Place this mix in a large bowl. In a smaller bowl, combine and stir:

2   eggs
$2/3$ cup apple cider
4   tablespoons melted butter
1   teaspoon vanilla

Mix together the dry and wet ingredients in the large bowl. Turn out the dough onto a floured surface. Pat to $1/2$ inch thickness. Cut with a donut cutter. Heat 2 inches of cooking oil to 350 degrees. Carefully place donuts into hot oil. Cook 3 to 4 minutes then turn and cook an additional 3 to 4 minutes. Yum!

SPICED
APPLE CIDER

Place this spice packet, still in its cheesecloth, in a large saucepan or slow cooker with:

2   quarts apple cider
1   quart water
1   orange, sliced

Heat until warm, but do not boil. Serve warm and sip a taste of something good!

Refrigerator
Biscuit
Donuts

Open the biscuits. With the neck of an empty pop bottle, make a hole in the center of each biscuit. Remove the "hole." Heat 2 inches of oil over medium-high heat in a deep skillet. Place 4 to 5 biscuits in the oil and cook 1 to 2 minutes. Turn, cook 1 to 2 minutes more or until lightly browned. Remove. Place each donut in a bag of sugar and shake, coating well. Place on paper towels to cool.

Apple Cider
DONUTS

Place this mix in a large bowl. In a smaller bowl, combine and stir:

2   eggs
$2/3$ cup apple cider
4   tablespoons melted butter
1   teaspoon vanilla

Mix together the dry and wet ingredients in the large bowl. Turn out the dough onto a floured surface. Pat to $1/2$ inch thickness. Cut with a donut cutter. Heat 2 inches of cooking oil to 350 degrees. Carefully place donuts into hot oil. Cook 3 to 4 minutes then turn and cook an additional 3 to 4 minutes. Yum!

Seasoned RICE

To prepare as a side dish, combine 2 cups of water and 1 tablespoon butter in a saucepan and bring to a boil. Stir in 1 cup of this rice mix.

Reduce heat; cover and simmer for 15 to 20 minutes. This makes $3\frac{1}{2}$ cups and serves six.

Seasoned RICE

To prepare as a side dish, combine 2 cups of water and 1 tablespoon butter in a saucepan and bring to a boil. Stir in 1 cup of this rice mix.

Reduce heat; cover and simmer for 15 to 20 minutes. This makes $3\frac{1}{2}$ cups and serves six.

ALL-DAY APPLE BUTTER

APPLE PIE JAM

Homestyle
STUFFING

Place the contents of this seasoning bag in a small saucepan with 1 cup water and 2 tablespoons butter. Bring to a boil and simmer for 10 minutes. Stir in cubed bread and mix well. Let sit for 5 minutes and serve, or place in the oven for the last 20 minutes of your turkey's cooking time.

Pumpkin Pecan Butter

HOMESTYLE STUFFING

Place the contents of this seasoning bag in a small saucepan with 1 cup water and 2 tablespoons butter. Bring to a boil and simmer for 10 minutes. Stir in cubed bread and mix well. Let sit for 5 minutes and serve, or place in the oven for the last 20 minutes of your turkey's cooking time.

Turkey Noodle SOUP

This provides the perfect way to use some of that leftover turkey! In a large pot, sauté in $1/4$ cup butter until tender:

2   stalks celery, chopped
1   carrot, chopped
1   onion, chopped

Add 8 to 10 cups water, 4 cups turkey, and this mix. Simmer over medium heat until the split peas are tender, about 45 minutes.

TURKEY NOODLE
SOUP

This provides the perfect way to use some of that leftover turkey! In a large pot, sauté in $1/4$ cup butter until tender:

2   stalks celery, chopped
1   carrot, chopped
1   onion, chopped

Add 8 to 10 cups water, 4 cups turkey, and this mix. Simmer over medium heat until the split peas are tender, about 45 minutes.

Cranberry

Walnut

Relish

Marinated

Italian

Cheese

Oatmeal Christmas
Pancakes

To 2 cups of this mix, add and stir well (alternating the addition of oil and water):

2 eggs, beaten
⅓ cup oil
1 cup water

Pour batter by ¼ cupfuls onto a lightly greased hot griddle on medium-low heat. Turn after 2 minutes. Cook until second side is brown. This makes 10 pancakes per batch to wake those you love on Christmas Day with the delicious aroma of pancakes.

CRANBERRY WALNUT RELISH

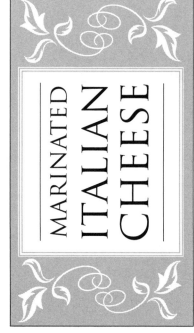

MARINATED ITALIAN CHEESE

Oatmeal Christmas
Pancakes

To 2 cups of this mix, add and stir well (alternating the addition of oil and water):

2 eggs, beaten
⅓ cup oil
1 cup water

Pour batter by ¼ cupfuls onto a lightly greased hot griddle on medium-low heat. Turn after 2 minutes. Cook until second side is brown. This makes 10 pancakes per batch to wake those you love on Christmas Day with the delicious aroma of pancakes.

CANDY CANE
✦✦
C A P P U C C I N O

Stir 1 tablespoon of this mix into 1 cup boiling water and enjoy.

 *Candy Cane Cappuccino*

Stir 1 tablespoon of this mix into 1 cup boiling water and enjoy.

GINGERBREAD MAN
Cookies

To this mix, combine the following that you've previously creamed together:

1 cup vegetable shortening
1 cup sugar
1 egg
1 cup molasses
2 tablespoons vinegar

Refrigerate dough for 2 to 3 hours. On a lightly floured surface, roll out dough to ⅛-inch thickness. Cut cookies with a gingerbread man cutter. Bake at 375 degrees for 5 minutes. Cool and decorate.

GINGERBREAD MAN
Cookies

To this mix, combine the following that you've previously creamed together:

1 cup vegetable shortening
1 cup sugar
1 egg
1 cup molasses
2 tablespoons vinegar

Refrigerate dough for 2 to 3 hours. On a lightly floured surface, roll out dough to ⅛-inch thickness. Cut cookies with a gingerbread man cutter. Bake at 375 degrees for 5 minutes. Cool and decorate.

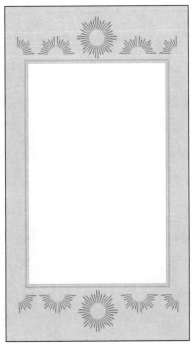

Chocolate Raspberry ⊰ *Spread* ⊱

Enjoy as an ice cream topping or over angel food cake.

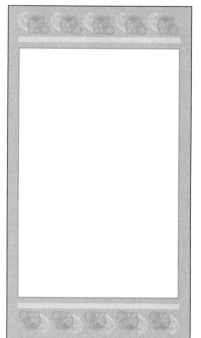

Chocolate Raspberry

S P R E A D

Enjoy as an ice cream topping or over angel food cake.

*"And now these
three remain:
faith, hope
and love.
But the greatest
of these is love."*

1 Corinthians 13:13

*"No eye has seen,
no ear has heard,
no mind has
conceived
what God has
prepared
for those
who love him."*

1 Corinthians 2:9

*"And now these three remain:
faith,
hope
and love.
But the greatest of these is love."*

1 Corinthians 13:13

*"No eye has seen, no ear has heard,
no mind has conceived
what God has prepared
for those who love him."*

1 Corinthians 2:9

"*Let your light shine before men, that they may see your good deeds and praise your Father in heaven.*"

Matthew 5:16

"Live a life of love, just as Christ loved us and gave himself up for us as a fragrant offering and sacrifice to God."

Ephesians 5:2

Be My Valentine

"*Let your light shine before men, that they may see your good deeds and praise your Father in heaven.*"

Matthew 5:16

"Live a life of love, just as Christ loved us and gave himself up for us as a fragrant offering and sacrifice to God."

Ephesians 5:2

Be My Valentine

"For I am convinced that neither death nor life, neither angels nor demons, neither the present nor the future, nor any powers, neither height nor depth, nor anything else in all creation, will be able to separate us from the love of God that is in Christ Jesus our Lord."

Romans 8:38–39

Merry, Cozy Christmas

"For to us a child is born, to us a son is given, and the government will be on his shoulders. And he will be called Wonderful Counselor, Mighty God, Everlasting Father, Prince of Peace."

Isaiah 9:6

"For I am convinced that neither death nor life, neither angels nor demons, neither the present nor the future, nor any powers, neither height nor depth, nor anything else in all creation, will be able to separate us from the love of God that is in Christ Jesus our Lord."

Romans 8:38–39

Merry, Cozy Christmas

"For to us a child is born, to us a son is given, and the government will be on his shoulders. And he will be called Wonderful Counselor, Mighty God, Everlasting Father, Prince of Peace."

Isaiah 9:6

ACKNOWLEDGMENTS

This all started with a thoughtful present for a pig-tailed little girl who loved Laura Ingalls Wilder—a Christmas gift of red mittens, a shiny new penny, a rag doll named Charlotte, and a copy of the book *Little House in the Big Woods*.

A basket of these gifts like Laura received sparked an idea that grew into a workshop complete with a simple handout.

We continue to be amazed as we look back at how that gift idea handout and workshop became a self-published book, and finally the lovely edition you now hold in your hands. We're three stay-at-home moms, each gifted in different ways but with a common desire—to encourage women in their gift giving. So many people encouraged us along the way. Thank you to:

- Hearts at Home National Ministry—Jill Savage for having the vision to provide a conference with encouraging workshops for moms, and Dee Kirwan for allowing us to serve as speakers in this ministry.
- Kelly's MOPS group at Calvary Baptist Church in Canton, Michigan: Thanks for giving us our very first invitation to share our ideas with moms.
- Karen & Trish's Mug & Muffin Moms group at First Baptist Church in St. Johns, Michigan: Thanks for being our taste testers, sounding board, and enthusiastic cheerleaders.
- Our circle of friends, especially Dorothy W., Karen L., Tammy U., and Sherry N.—you were always ready with red pen to proofread, wooden spoon to field test, and pom-poms to encourage us to keep going.

- Authors Jonni McCoy, Emilie Barnes, Sheri Torelli, and Donna Otto. How we appreciate your willingness to share your knowledge of the publishing process with us and for helping to promote our book!

- Jeanette Thomason, Cheryl Van Andel, Kim Boldt, Dan Malda, Mary Wenger, and all of those at Fleming H. Revell and our Baker Book House family. We're grateful to you for taking a chance on three unknown Michigan moms, and for your guidance and support as we open this new chapter in our lives.

INDEX

These three Michigan moms began Homespun Gifts from the Heart workshops six years ago for churches and women's groups, including Mothers of Preschoolers International (MOPS). Collectively, they've taught in public schools as well as at home, contributed to magazines, won sewing and quilting and cooking awards, served as pastor's wives, counseled youth, taught Bible school, coached cheerleaders, created women's events (deep breath)—but not all in the same day!

Karen Ehman admits she's the "hopelessly craft-challenged one" in the trio, though she enjoys baking and cooking and has won several blue ribbons at various county fairs. She's a graduate of Spring Arbor College, the wife of Todd, and the homeschooling mother of their three children. As a frequent speaker to moms groups, Karen's a regular contributor to Hearts at Home's monthly magazine and devotional, is the founder of Lansing's Mug and Muffin Mom's Night Out for at-home moms, and has been a workshop leader at regional and national mothers conferences every year since 1997. Before motherhood, Karen was a teacher and cheerleading coach.

Kelly Hovermale, the Craft Queen and the natural seamstress of the group, is Westland Michigan's 1999 Mother of the Year. With a master's degree in elementary education, she taught third grade for several years after marrying Greg; she now homeschools their three sons and one daughter. She's passionate about challenging women to weave literature into their gift-giving ideas and is active in the homeschooling community as a speaker and mentor. She is the founder and former coordinator of a MOPS group at her church in suburban Detroit.

Trish Smith loves to work on the computer and inspired her friends to make this book with adorable gift tags and labels on the countless handmade gifts she makes for family and friends. Before marrying Doug and homeschooling their son, Trish attended Western Michigan University and worked in both floral and fabric industries. Today she spends much of her time with children: teaching homeschooled girls to sew, leading a Boy Scout troop, and coordinating craft time for her church's Vacation Bible School. In her spare time, she loves listening to and making music, sewing, quilting, crafting, and finding ways to make her home a haven for her family.

Do you have a Homespun Gift idea of your own that you'd like to share? How about one particularly for kids—to be fashioned by kids? Or one that is perfect to give to a child?

Mail ideas to the authors at Homespun Gifts, P.O. Box 484, St. Johns, MI 48879, and they may use it in one of their national workshops or another edition of the book *Homespun Gifts from the Heart*. Submissions should be sent with permission to pass along the idea, helping other women help each other. Also, check out the authors' site at www.homespun-hearts.com